AF600383

Power, Constraint, and Policy Change

SUNY series in American Constitutionalism

Robert J. Spitzer, editor

Power, Constraint, and Policy Change

Courts and Education Finance Reform

Robert M. Howard
Christine H. Roch
Susanne Schorpp
Shane A. Gleason

Published by State University of New York Press, Albany

Printed in the United States of America

For information, contact State University of New York Press, Albany, NY
www.sunypress.edu

Library of Congress Cataloging-in-Publication Data

Names: Howard, Robert M., 1956– author. | Roch, Christine H., author. | Schorpp, Susanne, author. | Gleason, Shane A., author.
Title: Power, constraint, and policy change : courts and education finance reform / Robert M. Howard, Christine H. Roch, Susanne Schorpp, and Shane A. Gleason.
Description: Albany : State University of New York Press, 2021. | Series: SUNY series in American constitutionalism | Includes bibliographical references and index.
Identifiers: LCCN 2020024650 | ISBN 9781438481357 (hardcover : alk. paper) | ISBN 9781438481371 (ebook)
Subjects: LCSH: Public policy (Law)—United States—States. | Courts—United States—States. | Education—United States—States—Finance.
Classification: LCC KF4695 .H69 2021 | DDC 344.73/076—dc23
LC record available at https://lccn.loc.gov/2020024650

10 9 8 7 6 5 4 3 2 1

Robert Howard dedicates this book to his family, past, present, and future. To my late Mom and Dad, Nana and Papa, Grandma and Grandpa, I miss you and will always love you. To my now four wonderful children, Courtney, Jordan, Dave, and Kate, and to my grandchild, Arthur, you make everything I do worthwhile. Finally, to the love of my life and companion for over forty years, Taryn, if you had not allowed a disgruntled thirty-something lawyer to start a new career, none of this would have been possible.

Christine Roch dedicates this book to her family. To my wonderful husband—who has done a tremendous job of supporting what I do and in being there with me through both great times and difficult ones. And to my beautiful, smart, and funny daughter whom I am so lucky to have. I also am thankful for the love, support, and encouragement that I have received throughout the years from my parents and my sister.

Susanne Schorpp dedicates this book to Ella.

Shane Gleason dedicates this book to Alex, his favorite teacher.

Contents

Figures and Tables

Figures

Tables

Acknowledgments

This book was many years in the making and relied on help and advice from numerous people. We know we will omit some names who deserve mention—memories have a way of fading. However, we will do our best. First, we would like to thank the late Susette Talarico of the University of Georgia. Susette encouraged us to submit a very early and very preliminary analysis of courts and education policy to the *Justice System Journal* and took two very junior colleagues under her wing to help us produce a publishable article. She is missed.

We would also like to thank the editors and the various anonymous reviewers of the journals that published earlier versions of our research: in particular, Cornell Clayton and Amy Mazur of *Political Research Quarterly*; Nancy Reichman of *Law and Policy*; and Joseph O'Rourke, the student editor-in-chief of the *Albany Law Review*, all of whom helped us immensely as we worked our way through this vast literature and data and tried to offer some helpful ideas on state courts and education finance reform.

The authors wish to acknowledge all the research assistance by graduate students through the years, many of whom have gone on to have outstanding academic careers and others who will have wonderful careers: Shenita Brazelton, Jeffery Glas, Diana White, Morgan Smith, Jeffrey Davis, and Pamela Corley.

Chapter 1

Introduction

The Fight over Funding

The Kansas Constitution has a provision providing for a free public education. Article 6, section 1 of the constitution states, "The legislature shall provide for intellectual, educational, vocational and scientific improvement by establishing and maintaining public schools, educational institutions and related activities which may be organized and changed in such manner as may be provided by law." Article 6, section 6 spells out the financing:

> (a) The legislature may levy a permanent tax for the use and benefit of state institutions of higher education and apportion among and appropriate the same to the several institutions, which levy, apportionment and appropriation shall continue until changed by statute. Further appropriation and other provision for finance of institutions of higher education may be made by the legislature.
>
> (b) The legislature shall make *suitable* provision for finance of the educational interests of the state. *No tuition shall be charged* for attendance at any public school to pupils required by law to attend such school, except such fees or supplemental charges as may be authorized by law. The legislature may authorize the state board of regents to establish tuition, fees and charges at institutions under its supervision.

In 2011, Sam Brownback became governor of Kansas. Along with allies in the Kansas state legislature, Brownback pushed through a series of significant tax cuts, created as part of a "real, live experiment" in governance (Berman 2015), designed to stimulate the state economy and result in an expansion of state revenue. Instead, the state has seen a significant decline in revenue and a downgrade in the state's credit rating (Hanna 2016). The decline in revenue has led to severe cutbacks in state spending, including education. Specifically, Brownback and the Republican-dominated legislature changed the way funds were allocated to public schools. Previously, money had been allocated on a per pupil basis to ensure adequate financing for each district. This time Brownback and the legislature passed a block grant provision providing a set amount of funds to each district, leaving in doubt whether all school districts were to receive "suitable provision" for financing public education.

When subsequent litigation reached the state supreme court, the court, relying on a state court precedent, held that the block grant provision did not provide enough financing for each district's education requirements. The court ordered the state to increase education funding and distribute its money without creating major funding differences between poor and rich districts.

While the Kansas high court ordered the legislature to remedy inequities in the school finance system, it refrained from opining on the adequacy (or suitability) issue, sending the case back to the lower courts. The following May, the legislature added $129 million into the finance system targeted at property-poor districts, thus fulfilling its court-ordered equity obligation. However, at the end of the year in 2014, a lower court three-judge panel ruled that the finance system plan was still inadequate, potentially forcing the governor to roll back his signature tax cuts in order to increase school spending.

In response, Brownback and the more conservative members of the legislature enacted retaliatory measures designed to limit the court's authority, including a measure to increase the definition of an impeachable offense to include "attempting to subvert fundamental laws and introduce arbitrary power" and "attempting to usurp the power of the legislative or executive branch of government" (Lefler 2016).

In addition, the legislature curtailed the centralized authority of the supreme court over state court administration. The measure allows local courts to opt out of state supreme court control over budget preparation and submission and takes away the supreme court's authority to pick chief district court judges.

In June of 2016, the legislature finally agreed to a compromise acceptable to plaintiffs and defendants in the court case, pending a definitive ruling by the state supreme court. The bill reinstates an earlier formula for distributing equalization aid, and it adds $38 million to that formula to fund education and avoid shortages. The state supreme court has yet to rule on the constitutionality of the provisions designed to weaken court authority.

Kansas is far from the only state to experience tension between the legislative, executive, and judicial branches of government. In 2003, for example, in Nevada, the legislature was required by the Nevada Constitution to approve a balanced budget, including funding for education, by a certain date. A recent amendment to the constitution also mandated a two-thirds majority of the house to pass a bill that would generate public revenue in any form, such as taxes.

The legislature failed to provide funding for education, because it was unable to get the two-thirds majority. Because of this, teachers had not been hired, programs were cut, and schools were not able to plan for the upcoming school year. Due to the impending financial crises, the governor therefore asked the court to compel the legislature to fulfill its constitutional duty to pass a balanced budget, including appropriations for education.

Subsequently, in *Guinn v. Angle* (2003)[1] the Nevada Supreme Court held that the two-thirds vote requirement was a procedural matter, which clashed with a substantive right, funding for education. The court held that the legislature had failed to fulfill the constitutional mandate because of conflict between provisions within the constitution and therefore found that it was the judiciary's responsibility to intervene. The court ruled that education is a basic constitutional right in Nevada, and that, "when a procedural requirement that is general in nature prevents funding for a basic, substantive right, the procedure must yield." The court ordered the legislature to pass a budget.

The decision proved controversial. Though the legislature adhered to the court's decision and approved education funding, the decision prompted outrage to the point that state assembly member Sharon Angle mounted an effort to unseat the state supreme court justices for what she and other members of the legislature viewed as an unconstitutional usurpation of power. One member of the legislature who voted with the majority was up for reelection and subsequently was defeated. With the retirement of three other justices who voted to defy the legislature, the majority coalition for the opinion did not exist any longer. Eventually, *Guinn* was overruled in 2006 in *Nevadans for Nevada v. Beers* (2006).[2] Here the court concluded that the Nevada Constitution should be read as a whole, to give effect to and harmonize each provision.

These cases represent one of the fundamental policy issues in American society, pitting the importance of education against the cost of funding this core American value. This debate repeats itself over a variety of critical domestic issues, whether it concerns entitlement spending or the cost of national defense or even funding for parks, library, and local services. Public opinion surveys consistently show strong support for Social Security, Medicare, national defense, and local services. However, just as often the public rejects measures designed to raise revenue for these ventures.

The debate over education funding provides insight into how the political system, particularly the courts, reacts to and deals with public policy when confronted with a core program that needs a method of taxpayer-funded revenue. Through the prism of education finance, scholars and those interested in both this specific issue and other great policy debates can examine the unique aspects of the American political system, and how and why courts often end up determining and resolving these debates. In many ways, education finance pivots around the fundamental parameters of American political life. Education finance deals with important issues of tax and spending, federalism, and the interplay of the separated powers in both the state and federal systems. Education financing has involved governors, legislatures, and, of course, courts on both state and federal levels. It has at times pitted the courts against these other institutions. Education funding has involved the federal constitution and, most importantly for our purposes, the state constitutions as well as legislation and court-mandated remedies, equal protection and the guarantee of a free public education, the meaning of specific statutory and constitutional language, and ultimately who pays for this important value and how we should pay for this.

A Brief History of Public Education

Without a doubt, education plays a key role in American society and is highly valued. James Madison famously noted, "A well instructed people alone can permanently be a free people" (1810). Thomas Jefferson wrote that society needs to "educate and inform the whole mass of the people . . . they are the only sure reliance for the preservation of our liberty." More recently, former president George H. W. Bush said, "Think about every problem, every challenge, we face. The solution to each starts with education" (1991).

Because of its importance, free publicly financed education has been paramount to the attainment of so many goals promulgated in American public discourse. Earl Warren, writing in *Brown v. Board of Education* (1954), eloquently wrote:

> Today, education is perhaps the most important function of state and local governments. Compulsory school attendance laws and the great expenditures for education both demonstrate our recognition of the importance of education to our democratic society. It is required in the performance of our most basic public responsibilities, even service in the armed forces. It is the very foundation of good citizenship. Today it is a principal instrument in awakening the child to cultural values, in preparing him for later professional training, and in helping him to adjust normally to his environment. In these days, it is doubtful that any child may reasonably be expected to succeed in life if he is denied the opportunity of an education.[3]

Brown v. Board of Education represented a significant milestone in the understanding of the importance of education in modern society. While concerned with whether school desegregation violated the Equal Protection Clause of the United States Constitution, the opinion went much further than merely declaring segregation in public education unconstitutional. Chief Justice Warren, in the unanimous opinion, noted the key role public education plays in American life. Furthermore, the court argued that it could not turn the clock back to 1868, the year of the adoption of the Fourteenth Amendment, nor even to 1896, the year the Supreme Court issued its decision in *Plessy v. Ferguson*[4] upholding state-mandated segregation, when assessing the effects of segregation. Instead, to Warren and his brethren it was only relevant to consider public education in light of its present place in American life.

While education might be increasingly important in modern society, as the Madison, Jefferson, and Bush quotes demonstrate, the United States has long recognized the importance of free public education and, over time, the importance of financing public education. The importance even predates the existence of the United States. Massachusetts opened taxpayer-financed schools in the seventeenth century and by the time of the American Revolution many other colonies had at least partially funded public schools. Political elites began to support public-funded education. For example, John Adams in 1785 wrote, "The whole people must take upon themselves the education of the whole people and be willing to bear the expenses of it. There should not be a district of one mile square, without a school in it . . . maintained at the public expense of the people themselves" (1785, 540).

In 1790, the Commonwealth of Pennsylvania established free public schools for the poor. The first public high school started in Boston in 1821, and by 1827 Massachusetts made all public schools free of charge. By the 1840s, according to census data, about 55 percent of 3.69 million children of school age attended local primary schools (Tucker 1843, chap. 6). To be sure, the education of African Americans was still sorely lacking. Slaves received almost no formal instruction, and after 1830 Southern states passed laws that prohibited the teaching of slaves. Free blacks, even in the North, were in segregated schools, and Southern schools remained segregated by law until *Brown v. Board of Education*. However, for white school-age children, even girls, things were different. As one scholar notes, "by the middle of the nineteenth century U.S. schooling rates were exceptionally high, schooling was widespread among the free population, and literacy was virtually universal, again among the free population" (Goldin 1999).

Educational innovation soon followed initial public schooling. With Massachusetts and famed educator Horace Mann leading the way, states adopted age-appropriate grading and age-appropriate classes. The day of the one-room schoolhouse with multiple grades in the same room was passing. Other changes included professionalized teaching, standardized curricula, and eventually mandated compulsory attendance throughout the nineteenth and early twentieth centuries.

By the 1870s, in recognition of the importance of free schooling, every state enacted a provision in their respective constitutions that guaranteed some form of free public education. However, guaranteeing free public education, what constitutes an adequate free public education, and then paying for it are distinct and separate issues. The sporadic movement toward free public education over two centuries also meant a lack of any coherent or universally accepted funding mechanism.

Tellingly, public schools were under local control with little or no state control or federal oversight or input. In addition to local control, the schools were generally locally financed. In fact, "federal aid was basically non-existent until 1917" (Benson and O'Halloran 1987, 504). Initially, localities funded schooling through a variety of measures, including taxes on whiskey. However, as free public schooling gained acceptance, particularly in northern states, the requirement of payment by parents who could afford to pay for schooling was abolished. This occurred first in the northern states, then in the western states, and finally the southern states.

The progressive movement of the latter part of the nineteenth century led to adoption of local taxation that met the basic cost of teacher salaries and school supplies. This meant the implementation of a taxation system on locally owned private property for the benefit of local schools as the dominant method to finance public schools. From the onset of universal free public education throughout the United States in the latter part of the nineteenth century and through the first three decades of the twentieth, property taxes on homes and commercial property were the primary revenue source for school funding. Over a forty-year period from 1890 through 1930 local funding of public education accounted for more than 80 percent of total public school revenue. State taxes funded the remainder.

The local or township model of school organization, begun in New England, became the model for public school organization. Other states followed this model initially centered on towns and cities. Those states with even more rural, smaller populations created even smaller jurisdictions. By the early 1930s, when the Office of Education first counted school districts, there were almost 130,000 separate school districts in the United States. While some had tax rates set by larger governing units, such as counties or townships, most were fiscally independent. Thus, even by the third decade of the twentieth century, the United States had an enormous number of school districts with independent fiscal decision-making powers.

However, the onset of the Great Depression in 1929 and 1930 imperiled local financing. The depression led to high unemployment and high foreclosure rates on homes, resulting in drops in property values and a subsequent significant decline in local revenue. This resulted in the first shift toward greater state financing of education. The post–World War II baby boom put additional stress on local financing and led to another jump in state aid. Finally, in the 1970s, taxpayer revolts against property taxes and the movement toward court-ordered finance reform led to the next increase in state aid to local schools. By the early 1980s, state support of schools independent of local financing amounted to close to 50 percent of revenue while the federal share was 6 percent (Benson and O'Halloran 1987, 506). This financing pattern continues through the present with almost one-half (46%) of primary and secondary public education funding throughout the United States coming from local funding (Snyder and Dillow 2011, 67), and the balance from state and federal sources.

The Funding Disparity and the Turn to Court-Ordered Solutions

When you rely on local funding for close to one-half of all public education funding, the result is that in the United States education spending is not equal. There is often significant disparity in the resources available and money spent for schools within any particular state as well as across states (Evans, Murray, and Schwab 1997; Wood and Theobald 2003). Since public education is financed chiefly through local revenue, and most of that revenue derives from taxes on commercial and residential property, this means that the funding that is available throughout most states varies considerably from state to state and from district to district within each state. There is significant expenditure variation between states and districts and not all of it can be attributed to cost differentials between the states. For example, in the school year 1993–1994, the state of New Jersey spent over $9,400 per pupil, while Utah spent one-third of that amount. New Jersey, on average, paid $17,000 in salary per teacher more than Utah paid.

Significant variation exists not only between states but also within states. When revenue is dependent to a large extent on property taxes that means revenue depends on property values. Areas with better, more expensive homes and a greater number of taxable businesses will have a larger property tax base to spend on education. A greater tax base means more spending on public schools, and more spending on public schools usually translates to better opportunities and better teachers at those schools. Figure 1.1 shows a map of the United States with spending per pupil by school district and demonstrates the disparity. The average spending per pupil in the United States is currently close to $12,000 per pupil. However, as the map shows, spending varies considerably.

The figure shows variation in spending from approximately one-third below the mean to one-third above. Certain states, such as New York and Connecticut, spend considerably above the national average. Other states, such as Florida, spend well below the national average. However, the figure clearly shows the disparity in funding within most states. In Texas, for example, most districts in the western part of the state spend above the mean, while the eastern part of the state lags far behind.

This emphasis on local funding sources and the resultant inequality of resources creates the classical problem of circularity. The single biggest determinant of housing values in a particular area is the quality of public schools in the area (Kane et al. 2006). The better the school, the higher the property values, and the higher the property values, the greater the property tax base and thus the larger the amount of money to spend on public education. This in turn creates better schools, which result in corresponding higher property values.

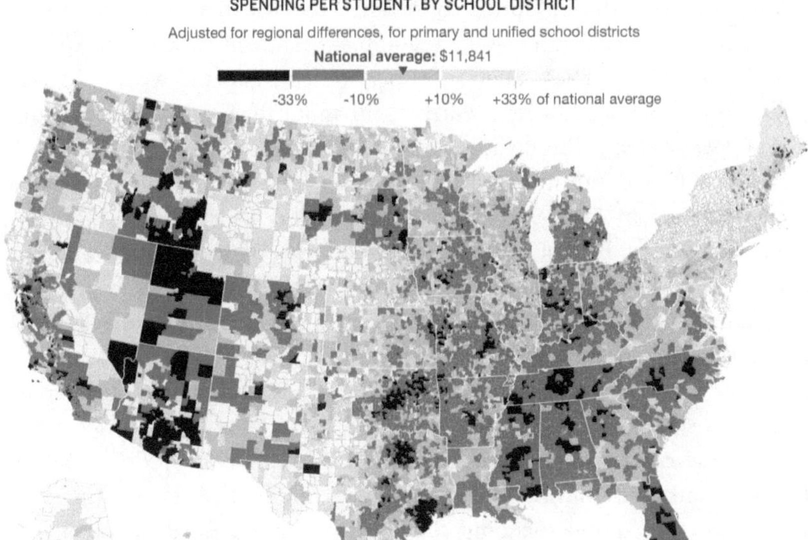

Figure 1.1. Spending per Pupil by School District US. (*Source:* Alyson Hurt and Katie Park/NPR. Data available through *Education Week*, U.S. Census Bureau. https://www.npr.org/2016/04/18/474256366/why-americas-schools-have-a-money-problem)

Even with the court's decision in *Brown v. Board of Education* and the subsequent commitment of the national government to educational equality, funding disparities made the goal of equal education seem distant and unobtainable for those students who attended schools in poor districts. These funding disparities created a form of unequal educational opportunity that *Brown* and its progeny could not solve. In an attempt to remedy this imbalance, those who have been unable to obtain legislative redress often turn to the courts.

There were some initial attempts at the state level to end the disparity. For example, in 1973 the New Jersey Supreme Court declared in *Robinson v. Cahill*[5] that New Jersey's school funding statute was unconstitutional because it violated the "thorough and efficient education" requirement of the state constitution. Similarly, in what is generally regarded as the first of the modern-era education finance litigation decisions, the Supreme Court of California, in 1971, ruled education a fundamental constitutional right in

Serrano v. Priest.[6] The California court noted the disparity in school funding between two school districts—the less affluent Baldwin Park Unified School District, which spent less than $600 per student, and the wealthy Beverly Hills Unified School District, which spent more than twice as much, over $1,200 per student. The justices noted that this more than 1 to 2 ratio in spending reflected the much greater 1 to 13 ratio of per student assessed property values in these two school districts. The justices noted that, even more disturbingly, Baldwin Park had a school property tax rate that was more than twice the rate of Beverly Hills. However, these school taxes produced less than half the amount of school expenditures. The California Supreme Court thus found the system of education finance in California violated the equal protection clause of the Fourteenth Amendment of the United States Constitution. This holding rested on the finding that district wealth violated the equal protection clause. In 1976, in *Serrano v. Priest* (*Serrano II*),[7] the same court affirmed the lower court's finding that the wealth-related disparities in per-pupil spending generated by the state's education finance system violated the equal protection clause of the California constitution.

The seminal early case in New Jersey relied on the state, not the federal, constitution. The New Jersey Constitution, article 8, section 4, paragraph 1, states, "The legislature shall provide for the maintenance and support of a thorough and efficient system of free public schools." In *Robinson*, plaintiffs challenged the New Jersey school finance system under the state equal protection clause, arguing that the "thorough and efficient" clause made education a fundamental interest and, directly under the education clause, arguing that the state failed to meet the guarantee of a *thorough and efficient* education in property-poor districts. The trial court found the New Jersey system unconstitutional under both the education and equal protection clauses of the state constitution. In a unanimous ruling affirming the decision, the Supreme Court of New Jersey relied on the education provision of the state constitution and found that plaintiffs had been denied "a thorough and efficient education." However, the court refused to find a denial of equal protection, a finding that would be buttressed in subsequent state cases. One scholar notes, "The court was concerned that basing its decision on the equal protection clause might implicate all municipal services. Unequal tax bases also result in some municipalities being able to provide better police and fire protection. If variations in local expenditures for education deny equal protection, then variations in local expenditures for other essential services may also deny equal protection to those living in poor municipalities" (Martell 1977, 149).

While these cases were at the state level, by far, the most potent attack on local funding of education occurred at the federal level premised on the use of the equal protection clause of the Fourteenth Amendment to the United States Constitution. This was the case of *San Antonio Independent School District v. Rodriguez* (1973). In an attempt to remedy funding disparities, a lawsuit was brought in the federal district court for the Western District of Texas in 1968 by members of the Edgewood Concerned Parent Association. The Edgewood school district was part of the greater San Antonio, Texas, school system. The parents represented their children and similarly situated students. In the initial complaint, the parents sued five other wealthier school districts, including Alamo Heights. Eventually the school districts were dropped from the case and the state of Texas became the sole defendant.

The parents argued that the "Texas method of school financing violated the equal protection clause of the Fourteenth Amendment to the U.S. Constitution." The lawsuit alleged, following the dictates of *Brown*, that education was a fundamental right and that wealth-based discrimination in the provision of education created in the poor, or those of lesser wealth, a constitutionally suspect class.

To support their argument, the plaintiffs offered data demonstrating the disparity between the Edgewood and Alamo Heights school districts. The wealthy Alamo Heights district spent on average $594.00 per pupil, while the poorer Edgewood district spent $356.00 per pupil. The greatest disparity came from local property tax revenue. Local revenue paid for $26.00 per pupil in Edgewood. This compared to $333.00 spent per pupil in Alamo Heights. Although Edgewood received more federal aid than Alamo Heights, this greater amount of federal aid could not compensate for the more than ten times disparity in available local funding. This led to enormous differences in resources and spending. For example, in the 1968–1969 school year:

> all of the Alamo Heights teachers had college degrees, while 80% of the Edgewood teachers had them; 37.17% of the Alamo Heights teachers had advanced degrees, while 14.98% of the Edgewood teachers had them; 11% of the Alamo Heights teachers depended on emergency teaching permits, while 47% of the Edgewood teachers depended on them; Alamo Heights' maximum teaching salary was 25% greater than Edgewood's maximum salary; Alamo Heights' teacher-student ratio was 1 to 20.5, while Edgewood's was 1 to 26.5; and Alamo Heights

> provided one counselor for every 645 students, while Edgewood provided one counselor for every 3,098 students. (Sutton 2008, 1967 citing brief of petitioner)

These disparities existed despite the fact that Edgewood property owners actually paid higher property tax rates. This paralleled the situation in California between the two disparate school districts. The property values in Edgewood were simply insufficient to cover the inequality with the wealthier district. After the plaintiffs won in a decision issued by a three-judge federal district court panel, the state appealed to the Supreme Court. The court did not hear arguments in the case until the fall of 1972 and the decision was not released until 1973.

The state of Texas was represented by Charles Alan Wright, a University of Texas law professor. Wright, who would later represent President Richard Nixon during the Watergate investigation, was a famed scholar of constitutional law and civil procedure and had extensive experience arguing before the Supreme Court. For Wright, the argument was simple: while acknowledging the disparity and admitting that the state should do a better job, there was simply no federal constitutional right to equal education. The equal protection clause did not apply to wealth and income, and thus wealth and income did not constitute any sort of protected class demanding greater Supreme Court scrutiny.

The US Supreme Court, in a narrow 5–4 decision and with the majority opinion authored by Justice Powell, agreed with the state of Texas and ruled that unequal financing for education did not violate the equal protection clause of the United States Constitution. Powell had at one time served on the Richmond Board of Education in Virginia. The opinion, while citing (and praising) *Brown v. Board of Education* and affirming the importance of education, ruled that education is not a fundamental right guaranteed in the Constitution. The opinion offered two rationales for the decision. First, according to Powell, "education, of course, is not among the rights afforded explicit protection under our Federal Constitution. Nor do we find any basis for saying it is implicitly so protected. As we have said, the undisputed importance of education will not alone cause this Court to depart from the usual standard for reviewing a State's social and economic legislation" (*Rodriguez*, 35). Because education is not a fundamental right, the court cannot subject the financing plan to strict scrutiny. Therefore, the state of Texas was free to enact a financing plan that rationally advanced its interests, even if that resulted in inequality among school districts.

In addition, the opinion failed to find "wealth" (or being poor) a protected class that would call for equal protection. Powell wrote:

> appellees have made no effort to demonstrate that it operates to the peculiar disadvantage of any class fairly definable as indigent, or as composed of persons whose incomes are beneath any designated poverty level. Indeed, there is reason to believe that the poorest families are not necessarily clustered in the poorest property districts. . . . Second, neither appellees nor the District Court addressed the fact that, unlike each of the foregoing cases, lack of personal resources has not occasioned an absolute deprivation of the desired benefit. The argument here is not that the children in districts having relatively low assessable property values are receiving no public education; rather, it is that they are receiving a poorer quality education than that available to children in districts having more assessable wealth. Apart from the unsettled and disputed question whether the quality of education may be determined by the amount of money expended for it, a sufficient answer to appellees' argument is that, at least where wealth is involved, the Equal Protection Clause does not require absolute equality or precisely equal advantages . . . (*Rodriguez*, 23–24)

Given this, the court did not find any federal constitutional violation in unequal financing schemes. That is, "the Constitution did not prohibit the government from providing different services to children in poor school districts than it did to children in wealthy school districts" (Van Slyke et al. 1994, 2). Politically, the Supreme Court outcome resulted from the retirement of several members of the Warren court and the election of Richard Nixon, who promised to appoint "strict constructionist" judges (Whittington 2003). The 1973 Burger court consisted of four justices appointed by President Richard Nixon: Chief Justice Warren Burger and Associate Justices Lewis Powell, Harry Blackmun, and William Rehnquist. They replaced Chief Justice Earl Warren and Associate Justices Black, Fortas, and Harlan, all of whom had served under Earl Warren as members of the Warren court. The Segal Cover scores,[8] which measure each justice's ideology through content analysis of newspaper editorials at the time of their confirmation (and run from 0 [most conservative] to 1 [most liberal]), for the four retired and the four replacement justices are represented in figure 1.2.

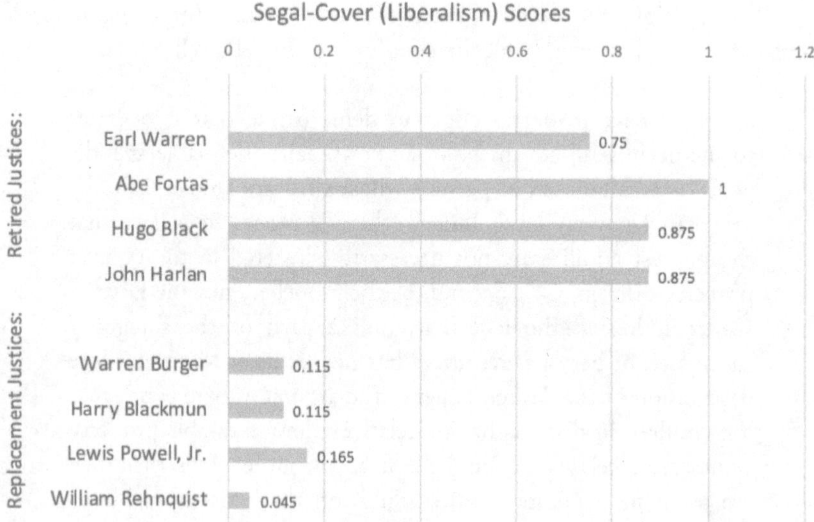

Figure 1.2. Ideology Scores for Retired Warren Court Justices and Replacement Burger Court Justices. (*Source:* http://www.stonybrook.edu/polsci/jsegal/qualtable.pdf)

The average ideology score for the four retired justices is .88, extremely liberal. The average ideology score for the four replacement justices is .11, very conservative. That is an average drop of more than .75, moving from liberal to conservative. Thus, much more conservative justices replaced some of the most liberal justices in the history of the United States Supreme Court and also replaced some of the most important members of the Warren court. It is true that justice ideology is not constant (Epstein et al. 1998) and that Harry Blackmun, whose voting record so matched his friend and fellow Minnesotan Warren Burger that the two were referred to as the "Minnesota Twins" (Yarbrough 2008, chap. 6), did significantly deviate from his early conservative voting record the longer he sat on the bench (Greenhouse 2005). However, at the time of the *Rodriguez* decision, Blackmun still had a more conservative voting record, matching that of his sponsor, Warren Burger.

These four relatively new justices, along with Justice Potter Stewart, a Republican Eisenhower appointee, constituted the Supreme Court majority in *Rodriguez* and voted in favor of the state of Texas, rejecting the argument of the parents; Justice Stewart also filed a concurring opinion. Four justices,

William O. Douglas, William Brennan, Thurgood Marshall, and Byron White, supported the school district.

Where *Brown* gave school districts and district courts the power to implement tools aimed at desegregation, *Rodriguez* denied the federal government means to address the underlying structure that creates and perpetuates segregation in schools. After decades of desegregation in the aftermath of *Brown* in the 1960s and 1970s, the 1990s and 2000s were marked by resegregation (Unah and Blalock 2019; Ogletree 2013). Reardon et al. (2012) find that the effects of "court-ordered desegregation plans . . . fade over time, at least in the South, where most of the districts under court order are located. Following the release from court order, white/black desegregation levels begin to rise within a few years of release and continue to grow steadily for at least 10 years" (899). As long as de facto residential and social segregation exists, the success of desegregation through busing and other tools sanctioned after *Brown* will be temporary.

At the same time, residential segregation itself is tied to the limitations that have been and continue to be placed on the tools courts have at their disposal to combat inequality and segregation. As Unah and Blalock write: "Anti-integration leaders discovered back in 1970 that if they could remove overt discussion of race from their rhetoric and label themselves as advocates of 'local control' and 'antibusing,' they could shift the narrative away from race. The Supreme Court has followed a similar tact, advocating that school districts find 'race-neutral' alternatives to promote diversity in schools" (2019, 4).

Federal involvement in equality as it regards education—whether in terms of race and ethnicity or in terms of funding—has weakened consistently with *Rodriguez* and *Brown*'s progenies in the 1990s and after. As a result, federal constitutional and legal tools were increasingly placed out of reach for reformers, which shifted the responsibility of addressing the interconnected web of economic and racial inequality to state laws and constitutions.

While *Rodriguez* effectively precluded any further court action at the federal level, it did not stop further court action at the state courts. If a state court ruling relies solely on interpretations of state constitutional law, then its decisions are unreviewable by the federal courts; as Justice William Brennan explained: "We are utterly without jurisdiction to review such state decisions" (1977, 501). State high courts of last resort are the supreme arbiters of state law. The principle laid down by the US Supreme Court in *Murdock v. City of Memphis* (1875) held that the US Supreme Court could not review a decision of a state high court unless it involved an application of federal law. This is the principle known as Adequate and Independent State Grounds. Put more simply, under the doctrine of Adequate and Independent State Grounds, state high court decisions that are based on state law and independent of federal interpretation are outside the jurisdiction of the federal courts and, thus, not reviewable by the US Supreme Court (Haas 1981; see *Michigan v. Long* [1983]). This of course presupposes that the state court decision does not intrude or lower civil liberties and rights already guaranteed under the United States Constitution.

In terms of educational financing, the doctrine of Adequate and Independent State Grounds means that the United States Constitution and the United States Supreme Court do not necessarily have the final say in how a state chooses to finance public education. Instead, if the state legislature fails to find an acceptable solution to school funding, litigants can turn to state constitutions and state courts for remedies. This doctrine then precludes the US Supreme Court from even reviewing the state high court's decision if the state high court's decision is premised solely on its own laws and own state constitution.

While California and New Jersey were the first states to have litigation over education finance, these cases continue until today. As of December 2015, forty-four states have experienced some form of state education finance litigation. In figure 1.3, we show the states and the litigation with cases starting in 1971 through 2010. The map shows that all but a few states have experienced education finance reform litigation. Plaintiffs have successfully challenged those states in medium gray, while school districts and states have won where the color is dark gray. A few states have had mixed results.

Why Courts? A Theory of Policy Change through State Courts

Of course, all this begs the question, why courts, and how do courts move social and public policy? Given attitudinal preferences of judges throughout the federal and state courts, we next want to present a theory of how judges make policy, that is, how they operate within the American political system. We make no argument that courts are more important than elected officials in making policy, but we do argue that they perform an important and influential role. In this section we offer a theory of how courts make

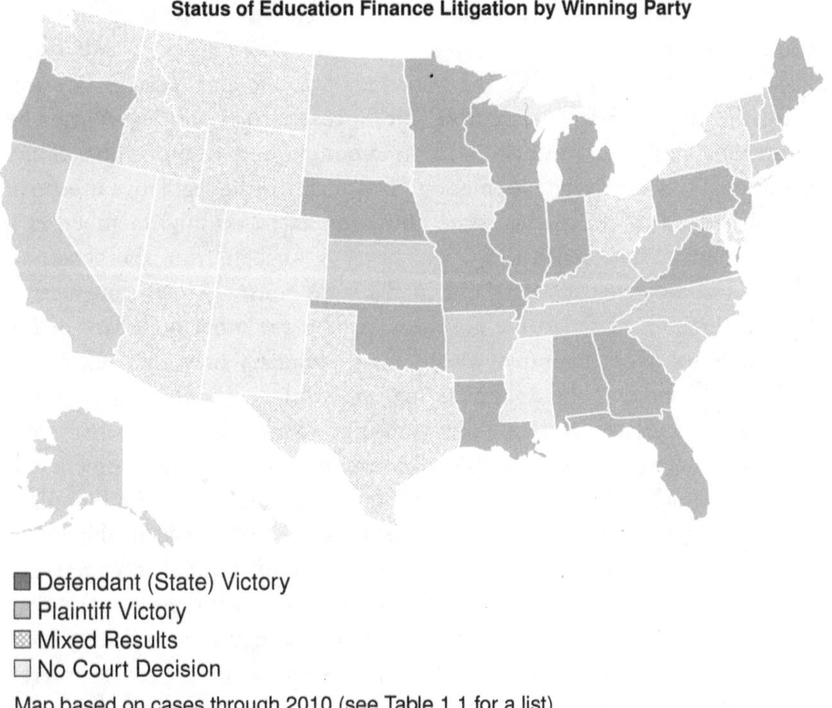

Figure 1.3. Status of Education Finance Litigation by Winning Party. (*Source:* National Education Access Network http://schoolfunding.info/litigation-map/Figure)

policy that borrows from prior works by Howard and Nixon (2002) and Howard and Steigerwalt (2011), who use Hammond and Knott's (1996) articulation of agency control which they expand to the concept of policy control. For our purposes, we examine state courts.

In this formulation, courts exogenously establish a "legal set." The legal set may or may not overlap with what is termed the "legislative-executive core." The legislative-executive core is the critical veto point over executive action; in other words, policies falling within this core are supported by both the legislature and the executive while policies falling outside the core are those that run the risk of being vetoed by the governor or overridden by the state legislature. One assumes therefore that this core point on a liberal-conservative continuum is where most policy will be set at the state level if one substitutes a governor for the executive. We present this situation in figure 1.4.

Figure 1.4 implies that the majority of public and social policy will fall within the "legislative-executive core," because such policies will not be overturned through statutory means (Hammond and Knott 1996). If the governor, **G**, is relatively extreme, one boundary of the legislative-executive core is defined by the median state house (or state assembly) member, $\mathbf{H_m}$, or the median state senator, $\mathbf{S_m}$, whichever is furthest from the governor. The crucial veto-override legislator in the state house, $\mathbf{H_{vo}}$, or state senate, $\mathbf{S_{vo}}$, whichever is closer to the governor, defines the other boundary of the core. It is the views captured within these boundary lines that reflect the policy preferences of the dominant state political coalition.

If the legal set does not fully subsume the legislative-executive core, then judicial review presents additional constraints on policy development and change. In such a situation, policy will not be established at the boundary of the legislative-executive core, because it will be overturned in the courts and then a court-ordered policy will be substituted for the elected preferences anywhere within the legal set. Alternatively, if the state supreme court's policy preference falls outside of the preferences of the legislative-executive core, then there is the possibility of a legislative override of the court-ordered policy. Statutory interpretation policies established by the courts are easier

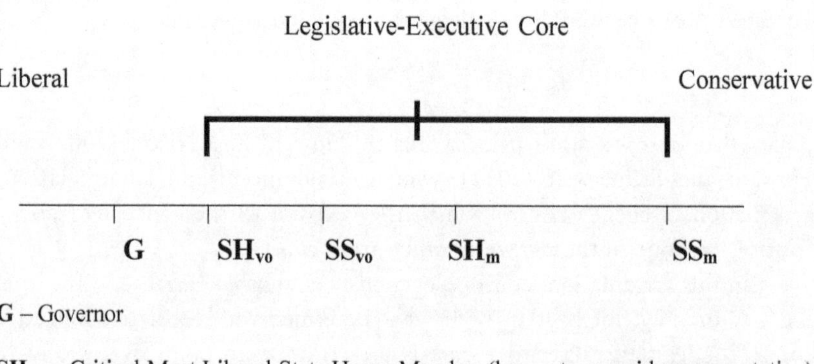

G – Governor

$\mathbf{SH_{vo}}$ – Critical Most Liberal State House Member (key veto override representative)

$\mathbf{SS_{vo}}$ – Critical Most Liberal State Senator (key veto override senator)

$\mathbf{SH_m}$ – Median State House Member

$\mathbf{SS_m}$ – Median State Senator

Figure 1.4. Policy Domain without State Supreme Courts.

for the legislature to override than constitutional interpretations. We show this added legal set for state supreme courts in figure 1.5.

How does a state supreme court establish a range of permissible policy outcomes? Consider figure 1.6's illustration of a five-judge state supreme court, $J_{1\text{-}5}$, whose ideological preferences are arrayed on a liberal-conservative scale. The legal set here is established by J_3, the median judge. In this case, the legal set is relatively narrow and shows a more liberal court. The set represents the indifference points of the median justice's ideological preferences. Move

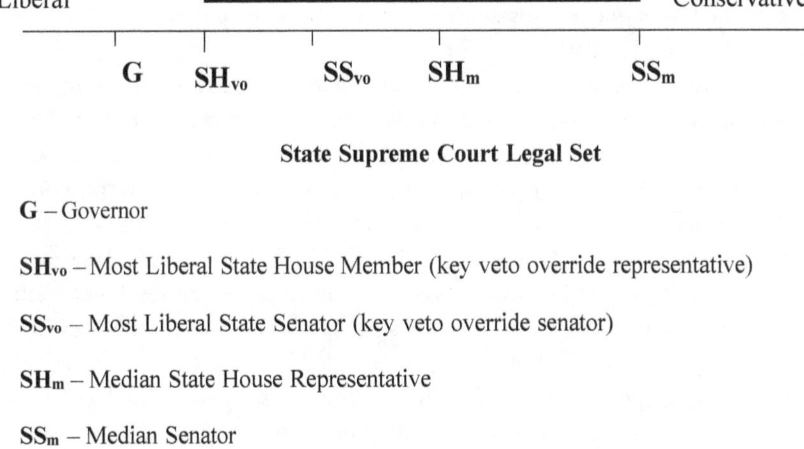

Figure 1.5. Policy Domain with State Supreme Courts.

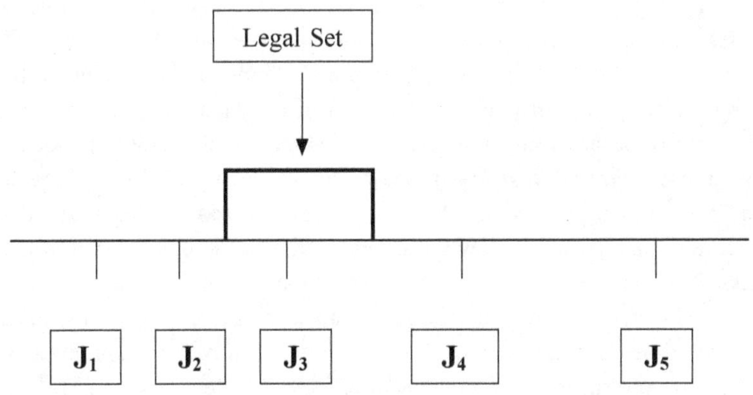

Figure 1.6. Policy Range of State Supreme Courts.

the median justice to the right or left and the legal set moves accordingly. Since state courts are either elected or appointed, or appointed subject to a retention election, it is reasonable to assume that the legal set will fall within or close to the legislative-executive core, particularly if the judge confronts reelection or a retention election. Therefore, when the elected officials are unable to act, the court can step in and enact policy somewhat close to elected official preferences.

The extension of these theories highlights how, even within a system of constraints, judicial decisions can still substantially impact policy. And, the more the views of the judges are in line with those of elected officials, the more power judges possess to substantially alter policy with little fear of oversight or backlash.

Furthermore, these models do not take into account the numerous instances when legislatures and executives decide to cede power over certain issue areas to the courts, thus increasing the courts' ability to influence state and national policy. In particular, legislatures might defer to the courts, thus transferring power to make important policy choices to the courts on certain issues (see, e.g., Graber 1993; Lovell 2003). For example, legislatures might pass laws that are intentionally vague in order to reach legislative compromise and, just as importantly, shift the blame for necessary difficult decisions to the courts. As Katzmann explains, "ambiguity [in statutes] is a deliberate strategy to secure a majority coalition in support of the legislation" (1997, 61). However, when those ambiguities inevitably lead to questions that must be resolved, courts are forced to answer the question, even if the legislature has provided relatively little guidance, since courts *must* answer all legal claims properly brought before them.

On the other hand, legislatures may also deliberately pass legislation in order to provoke a reaction from the courts. Take, for example, the debates surrounding the passage of the Flag Protection Act in 1989. The Supreme Court in 1985 in the case of *Texas v. Johnson* struck down a Texas law prohibiting flag burning as a violation of the First Amendment. While a majority of senators and representatives voted for this law, a majority of them also recognized that the law was likely unconstitutional. However, many members supported the law for strategic purposes: they wanted the Supreme Court to strike down the law, and thus hopefully mobilize the necessary support to pass a constitutional amendment. As Senator Kasten stated, "The matter before us tonight is an attempt to provide by statute, the protection our flag deserves. Given the decision of five Supreme Court justices that the statute in *Texas v. Johnson* violated the Constitution, I don't believe this vehicle will work. But I will support this effort until the Senate considers the constitutional amendment which will provide the protection the flag deserves."[9]

Finally, it is not uncommon for legislatures to pass laws that deliberately increase the ability of individuals to bring lawsuits and thus increase the possibility of ceding policy-making power to the courts. One of the fundamental provisions of the Civil Rights Act of 1964 was that it enabled individuals to file discrimination claims against public and private employers who failed to follow the act's directives. Congress and the states have passed similar laws that increase the ability of individuals to gain access to the courts and resolve legal disputes, and to consequently further the legislature's policy goals. And, by increasing the propensity of the courts to have to address questions of statutory (and potentially constitutional) interpretation, these legislative actions directly affect the level of influence courts are able to exert over the content of policy in the states. Thus, while legislatures have the power to reduce the influence of the judiciary, they also many times act deliberately to increase this influence for a variety of reasons.

Waves of Finance Reform

There are distinctions between the types of cases that have been brought over the more than forty-five years since the *Rodriguez* decision. Scholars of education finance reform and the courts often differentiate litigation and court decisions into three distinct periods called "waves" (Briffault 2006; Heise 1995a, 1995b; Thro 1990). It is important to note that there has been some disagreement over the extent to which these efforts at reform in fact can clearly be assigned to different waves, with some scholars arguing that there exists more overlap in these approaches than is commonly recognized (Briffault 2006). However, a review of the cases (set forth in table 1.1) does show some recognizable differences in these waves, as we demonstrate ahead, and we use these waves for much of our analysis.

In all, there have been 104 state court cases that have reached state-level appellate courts challenging some aspect of school funding. Several of these cases have reached the highest courts in the applicable state and several are still pending even today. Some of the newer cases represent new legal actions, while a number of the cases either seek enforcement of previous court opinions or orders, or additional legislative enactment of court rulings, or represent attempts to overturn previous court orders mandating

Table 1.1. State Cases by Year

State	Case	Outcome	Year
California	*Serrano v. Priest*, 5 Cal. 3d 584, 487 P.2d 1241	Plaintiff	1971
Arizona	*Shofstall v. Hollins*, 110 Ariz. 88, 515 P.2d 590	Defendant	1973
Michigan	*Milliken v. Green*, 390 Mich. 389, 212 N.W. 2d 711	Defendant	1973
New Jersey	*Robinson v. Cahill 62 N.J. 473, 303 A.2d 273*	Defendant	1973
Montana	*State ex rel. Woodahl v. Straub*, 161 Mont. 141, 520 P.2d 776	Defendant	1974
Washington	*Northshore Sch. Dist. No. 417 v. Kinnear*, 530 P.2d 178	Defendant	1974
Alaska	*Hootch v. Alaska State Operated School System*, 536 P.2d 793	Plaintiff	1975
Idaho	*Thompson v. Engelking*, 96 Idaho 793, 537 P.2d 635	Defendant	1975
Kansas	*Knowles v. State Bd. of Ed.*, 219 Kan. 271, 547 P.2d 699	Plaintiff	1976
Ohio	*Board of Education of Cincinnati v. Walter*, 390 N.E.2d 813	Defendant	1976
Oregon	*Olsen v. State*, 276 Or. 9, 554 P.2d 139	Defendant	1976
California	*Serrano v. Priest* (*Serrano II*), 20 Cal. 3d 25, 569 P.2d 1303, 141 Cal. Rptr. 315	Plaintiff	1977
Connecticut	*Horton v. Meskill*, 172 Conn. 615, 376 A.2d 359	Plaintiff	1977
Washington	*Seattle School District No. 1 v. State*, 585 P.2d 71	Plaintiff	1978
Pennsylvania	*Danson v. Casey*, 484 Pa. 415, 399 A.2d 360	Defendant	1979
West Virginia	*Pauley v. Kelly*, 162 W. Va. 672; 255 S.E.2d 859	Plaintiff	1979
Wyoming	*Washakie County School District v. Herschler*, 606 P.2d 310	Plaintiff	1980
Georgia	*McDaniel v. Thomas*, 248 Ga. 632, 285 S.E.2d 156	Defendant	1981
California	*Lujan v. Colorado State Board of Education*, 649 P.2d 1005	Plaintiff	1982
New York	*Bd. of Ed. Levittown Union Free Sch. Dist. v. Nyquist*, 57 N.Y.2d 127	Defendant	1982
Arkansas	*DuPree v. Alma School District*, 279 Ark. 340, 651 S.W.2d 90	Plaintiff	1983
Maryland	*Hornbeck v. Somerset County Bd. of Ed*, 295 Md. 597, 458 A.2d 758	Defendant	1983

State	Case	Outcome	Year
West Virginia	*Pauley v. Bailey*, 174 W. Va. 167, 324 S.E.2d 128	Plaintiff	1984
Connecticut	*Horton v. Meskill*, 195 Conn. 24, 486 A.2d 1099	Plaintiff	1985
New York	*Britt v. NC State Board of Education*, 320 N.C. 790, 361 S.E.2d 71	Defendant	1987
Oklahoma	*Fair School Finance Council of OK v. State*, 746 P.2d 1135	Defendant	1987
South Carolina	*Richland County v. Campbell*, 294 S.C. 346; 364 S.E.2d 470	Plaintiff	1988
West Virginia	*State ex rel. Bds. of Ed. v. Chafin*, 376 S.E.2d 113	Plaintiff	1988
Kentucky	*Rose v. Council for Better Education*, 790 S.W.2d 186	Plaintiff	1989
Montana	*Helena Elem. Sch. Dist. No. 1 v. State*, 236 Mont. 44, 769 P.2d 684	Plaintiff	1989
Texas	*Edgewood Independent Sch. Dist. v. Kirby*, 777 S.W.2d 391	Plaintiff	1989
Wisconsin	*Kukor v. Grover*, 148 Wis. 2d 469, 436 N.W.2d 568	Defendant	1989
New Jersey	*Abbot v. Burke*, 119 N.J. 287	Defendant	1990
Oregon	*Coalition for Equitable School Funding v. State*, 311 Ore. 300	Defendant	1991
Texas	*Edgewood II*, 804 S.W.2d 491	Plaintiff	1991
Texas	*Edgewood III*, 826 S.W.2d 489	Plaintiff	1992
Alabama	*Opinion of the Justices*, 624 So. 2d 107	Defendant	1993
Idaho	*Idaho Schools for Equal Educational Opportunity v. Evans,* 123 **Idaho** 573, 850 P.2d 724	Plaintiff	1993
Massachusetts	*McDuffy v. Secretary*, 415 Mass. 545, 615 N.E.2d 516	Plaintiff	1993
Minnesota	*Skeen v. State*, 505 N.W. 2d 299	Defendant	1993
New Hampshire	*Claremont School District v. Gov.* 138 N.H. 183, 635 A.2d 1375	Plaintiff	1993
New Hampshire	*Londonderry Sch. Dist. v. State of NH*, 154 N.H. 153, 907 A.2d 988	Plaintiff	1993
Nebraska	*Gould v. Orr*, 244 Neb. 163, 506 N.W.2d 349	Defendant	1993
Tennessee	*Tenn. Small School Systems v. McWherter*, 851 S.W.2d 139	Plaintiff	1993
Arizona	*Roosevelt Elementary School District No. 66 v. Bishop*, 179 Ariz. 233, 877 P.2d 806	Plaintiff	1994

continued on next page

Table 1.1. Continued.

State	Case	Outcome	Year
Kansas	*Unified School Dist. No. 229 v. State*, 256 Kan. 232, 885 P.2d 1170	Plaintiff	1994
Maine	*School Administrative District No. 1 v. Comm'r*, 659 A.2d 854	Defendant	1994
New Jersey	*Abbot v. Burke*, 136 N.J. 444, 643 A.2d 575	Defendant	1994
North Dakota	*Bismarck Public School District No. 1 v. State*, 511 N.W.2d 247	Plaintiff	1994
Virginia	*Scott v. Commonwealth*, 247 Va. 379; 443 S.E.2d 138	Defendant	1994
New York	*Campaign for Fiscal Equity v. State*, 86 N.Y.2d 307, 631 N.Y.S.2d 565	Plaintiff	1995
New York	*R.E.F.I.T v. Cuomo*, 86 N.Y.2d 279, 631 N.Y.S.2d 551	Plaintiff	1995
Rhode Island	*City of Pawtucket v. Sundlun*, 662 A.2d 40	Defendant	1995
Tennessee	*Tenn. Small School Systems v. McWherter*, 894 S.W. 2d 734	Plaintiff	1995
Texas	Edgewood IV, 917 S.W.2d 717	Plaintiff	1995
Wyoming	*Campbell County School District v. State*, 907 P.2d 1238	Plaintiff	1995
Arkansas	*Tucker v. Lake View School District No. 25*, 323 Ark. 693, 917 S.W.2d 530	Plaintiff	1996
Connecticut	*Sheff v. O'Neill*, 678 A.2d 1267, 678 A.2d 1267	Plaintiff	1996
Florida	*Coalition for Adequacy and Fairness in School Funding v. Chiles*, 680 So. 2d 400	Defendant	1996
Illinois	*Committee for Educational Rights v. Edgar*, 174 Ill. 2d 1, 672 N.E.2d 1178	Defendant	1996
Alabama	*Ex parte James*, 713 So.2d 869	Defendant	1997
Alaska	*Matanuska-Susitna Borough School District v. Alaska*, 931 P.2d 391	Plaintiff	1997
Arizona	*Hull v. Albrecht*, 190 Ariz. 520, 950 P.2d 1141	Defendants	1997
Michigan	*Durant v. State*, 456 Mich. 175, 566 N.W.2d 272	Defendant	1997
New Hampshire	*Claremont v. Governor*, 142 N.H. 462, 703 A.2d 1353	Plaintiff	1997
New Jersey	*Abbott v. Burke*, 149 N.J. 145, 693 A.2d 417	Defendant	1997
North Carolina	*Leandro v. State*, 346 N.C. 336, 488 S.E.2d 249	Plaintiff	1997

State	Case	Outcome	Year
Ohio	*DeRolph v. State*, 78 Ohio St.3d 193, 677 N.E.2d 733	Plaintiff	1997
Vermont	*Brigham v. State*, 166 Vt. 246, 692 A.2d 384	Plaintiff	1997
Arizona	*Hull v. Albrecht*, 192 Ariz. 34, 960 P.2d 634	Defendants	1998
Idaho	*Idaho Schools for Equal Educational Opportunity v. State*, 976 P.2d 913	Plaintiff	1998
Louisiana	*Charlet v. Legislature of the State of LA*, 713 So.2d 1199	Defendant	1998
New Jersey	*Abbott v. Burke*, 153 N.J. 480, 710 A.2d 450	Defendant	1998
Pennsylvania	*Marrero v. Commonwealth*, 702 A.2d. 956	Defendant	1998
Pennsylvania	*Pennsylvania Association of Rural and Small Schools v. Ridge*, 558 Pa. 374; 737 A.2d 246	Defendant Defendant	1998 1999
Illinois	*Lewis E. v. Spagnolo*, 186 Ill. 2d 198, 710 N.E.2d 798		
New Hampshire	*Claremont v. Governor* 144 N.H. 210, 744 A.2d 1107	Plaintiff	1999
South Carolina	*Abbeville County School Dist. #1 v. State of South Carolina*, 335 S.C. 58, 515 S.E.2d 535	Plaintiff	1999
New Jersey	*Abbott v. Burke*, 163 N.J. 95, 748 A.2d 82	Defendant	2000
Ohio	*DeRolph v. State*, 89 Ohio St.3d 1, 728 N.E.2d 993	Plaintiff	2000
Wisconsin	*Vincent v. Voight*, 614 N.W.2d 388	Defendant	2000
Alabama	*Siegelman v. Alabama Association of School Boards*, 819 So. 2d 568	Defendant	2001
Ohio	*DeRolph v. State*, 93 Ohio St.3d 309, 754 N.E.2d 1184	Plaintiff	2001
Wyoming	*Campbell County School District v. State*, 2001 WY 19, 19 P.3d 518	Defendant	2001
New Hampshire	*Claremont v. Governor*, 794 A.2d 744	Plaintiff	2002
Tennessee	*Tenn. Small School Systems v. McWherter*, 91 S.W.3d 232	Plaintiff	2002
Arizona	*Crane Elementary School District v. State of Arizona*, 205 Ariz. 584, 74 P.3d 258	Defendants	2003
Kansas	*Montoy v. Kansas*, 275 Kan. 145, 62 P.3d 228	Plaintiff	2003
New York	*Campaign for Fiscal Equity, Inc. v. State*, 100 N.Y.2d 893, 801 N.E.2d 326, 769 N.Y.S.2d 106	Plaintiff	2003

continued on next page

Table 1.1. Continued.

State	Case	Outcome	Year
Alaska	*Kasayulie v. State*, 110 P.3d 947	Plaintiff	2005
Idaho	*Idaho Schools for Equal Educational Opportunity v. State*, 142 Idaho 450 129 P.3d 1199	Plaintiff	2005
Maryland	*Bradford v. Maryland State Bd. of Ed.*, 387 Md. 353, 875 A.2d 703	Plaintiff	2005
Massachusetts	*Hancock v. Driscoll*, 443 Mass. 428, 822 N.E.2d 1134	Plaintiff	2005
Montana	*Columbia Falls Elem. Sch. Dist. No. 6 v. Montana*, 2005 MT 69, 326 Mont. 304, 109 P.3d 257	Plaintiff	2005
Texas	*West Orange-Cove Consolidated ISD v. Neeley*, 176 S.W.3d 746	Defendant	2005
Arkansas	*Lake View School District v. Huckabee*, 370 Ark. 139, 257 S.W.3d 879	Plaintiff	2007
Nebraska	*Nebraska Coalition for Educational Equity and Adequacy v. Heineman*, 273 Neb. 531, 731 N.W.2d 164	Defendant	2007
Oklahoma	*Oklahoma Education Association v. State*, 158 P.3d 1058	Defendant	2007
California	*Lobato v. State*, 218 P.3d 358	Plaintiff	2009
Illinois	*Bonner v. Daniels*, No. 49A02-0702-CV-00188	Defendant	2009
Indiana	*Bonner ex rel. Bonner v. Daniels*, 907 N.E.2d 516	Defendant	2009
Missouri	*Comm. for Ed. Equality v. State of Missouri*, 218 S.W.3d 417	Defendant	2009
New Jersey	*Abbott v. Burke*, 199 N.J. 140, 971 A.2d 989	Defendant	2009
Oregon	*Pendleton School District v. State of Oregon*, 345 Ore. 596, 200 P.3d 133	Defendant	2009
Connecticut	*Coalition for Justice in Education Funding, Inc. v. Rell*, 295 Conn. 240	Plaintiff	2010
Colorado	No cases by 2010		
Delaware	No cases by 2010		
Hawaii	No cases by 2010		
Iowa	No cases by 2010		
Mississippi	No cases by 2010		
Nevada	No cases by 2010		
New Mexico	No state court of last resort cases		
South Dakota	No cases by 2010		
Utah	No cases by 2010		

finance reform. While six states have seen no litigation, other states have seen multiple court cases.

Scholars typically identify the first wave as beginning in the late 1960s to early 1970s. During this first wave, opponents of unequal financing premised the remedy to inequality with the equal protection clause of the Fourteenth Amendment to the United States Constitution. However, as we have seen, in *San Antonio Independent School District v. Rodriguez* (1973), the US Supreme Court ruled that unequal financing for education did not violate the equal protection clause of the United States Constitution. The next series of cases rested primarily on state education clauses and state equal protection clauses. This second wave of cases began following the *Rodriguez* decision and lasted until 1989. The third wave focused on specific adequacy provisions of state constitutions and continues to the present day (Tang 2010; Gillespie 2010; Heise 1995a, 1995b; Thro 1990).

While the first wave failed to effect change in financing reform, some of the early phases of the second wave were also often unsuccessful because they relied on state constitution equal protections clauses. In *Olsen v. State*[10] the Oregon Supreme Court, while acknowledging the ability of the state supreme court to give greater protection under the state constitution's equal protection clause than afforded under the United States equal protection clause, specifically declined to find such a constitutional violation under the state constitution. While acknowledging the disparity in resources, the state supreme court refused to find that "the Equal Rights Clause has been violated." The court held that the need for local control and authority outweighs the need for equality in resources. This failure to find an equal protection violation was repeated in other states. For instance, the New York high court, the Court of Appeals, in *Board of Education of the Levittown Union Free School District v. Nyquist*,[11] rejected the plaintiff's assertion that education was a fundamental right. In *McDaniel v. Thomas*[12] the Georgia Supreme Court disallowed the plaintiff's claim that the state equal protection clause mandated equal school financing.

During the second wave, the arguments used by those challenging the financing systems began to shift. The efforts during latter part of the second wave and the third wave have been much more successful. In these lawsuits, plaintiffs shifted to using state constitutional education clauses. These clauses, in conjunction with state equal protections clauses, required states to create and maintain public school systems. Courts that had been reluctant to broadly interpret the equal protection clause were now "more likely to invalidate finance plans because it is limited to the education context" (Verstegen 1994, 248). An example of this is the case of *Rose v.*

Council for Better Education,[13] wherein under the state education constitutional clause, the Kentucky Supreme Court issued a final ruling declaring "Kentucky's entire system of common schools . . . unconstitutional" (31).

In the third wave, litigants have particularly focused on the adequacy phrases of these articles to insist that they require the state to fund an acceptable and adequate education. During this third wave a significant number of litigants have sued to force the political branches to carry out the specific adequacy mandates of prior court orders. It became more common for courts to find themselves in the position of enforcing their own decisions. During this wave one often sees repeat litigation in a specific state. The same parties that had filed suit in previous cases relitigate the matter to ensure that education in the state meets the mandated definition of "adequacy."

Plan of the Book

In the following chapters in our book we examine this state policy dynamic by addressing several key questions and attempting to bring together different literatures. There are several excellent books that analyze and examine education financing and state courts. *Courts as Catalysts: State Supreme Courts and Public School Finance Equity* by Matthew Bosworth (2001) uses case study to analyze court approaches to school financing. *Framing Equal Opportunity: Law and the Politics of School Finance Reform* by Michael Paris (2010) also uses cases studies. Data in *Courts as Policymakers: School Finance Reform Litigation* by Anna Lukemeyer (2003) ends in 1996 and the data focus is on one state, New York. *On Equal Terms: The Constitutional Politics of Educational Opportunity* by Douglas Reed (reissued in paperback 2003) examines judicial intervention into education financing from a federalism perspective but omits policy ideas such as diffusion and more modern uses of social network analysis to analyze the interplay of different state judiciaries.

In contrast, our book, using the most up to date data, provides a comprehensive examination of both the internal and external political environment within which courts operate. We use an initial state separation of powers argument and then examine how courts can use external reference and policy diffusion to aid in their ability to mold and shape policy. We build on this prior scholarship investigating the role of courts in producing or contributing to policy change regarding equity in school funding through systematic analyses that relate the dynamics between legislature, governors, courts, and public actors.

We also take part in the debate over courts and their ability to create social and public policy. In part as a response to Rosenberg's "Hollow Hope" (2008) argument that suggests judicial impotence, scholars have attempted to identify whether and how courts matter in driving equity reform (Reed 1998, 2001; Bosworth 2001; Wood and Theobald 2003; Paris 2010). Their findings largely echo Reed's (2001) conclusion that "the degree of change in school finance over the past twenty-five years in states where supreme courts have struck down the existing systems is rather substantial, especially given the constraints under which courts must operate" (2001, 16). Reed focuses on the institutional and social entrenchments that make reform so difficult and that "[enable] a relatively narrow band of actors to preserve both their influence in public education and the advantages they accrue under its existing design" (2001, 161). Analyzing a number of states and their reform attempts, he identifies the limits under which courts operate as defined by the weak constitutional mandate in transforming issues under local power and the structures underlying racial and class inequalities.

Our book operates within the window of opportunity that courts carve out to advance equity in school funding. In doing so, our book does not add to the list of already excellent case studies concerning education finance reform and we are not investigating the social impact of court-mandated reform. Instead, we aim to provide a large N study that identifies general patterns regarding the role of courts in the reform movement. Our interest lies not only in relationships within a state, but also across states, as we look to how courts use information provided by states that passed court-mandated education finance reform to dispose of their own reform litigation.

For that purpose, we combine scholarship on state courts, which largely explains judicial decision making as defined by limits imposed through judge preference, law, and institutional constraints (Hall 1992; Brace and Hall 1990, 1995; Hall and Brace 1999; Langer 2002) with scholarship on policy diffusion. Scholarly research and its assumption of the independence of state-level judicial decision making and policy impact stands in marked contrast to much of the literature on the state-level adoption of policy. This literature has shown that state legislatures often adopt policy that has previously been adopted by neighboring states. We show three examinations of the constraints these state courts confront in making education finance decisions, as well as the interdependence of these state high courts. Our plan is as follows.

CHAPTER 2: WHY COURTS?

Bosworth's (2001) account of court-mandated education finance reform in Texas, Kentucky, and North Dakota foreshadows our discussion in chapter 2 of the relationship between courts and legislatures. In particular, Bosworth discusses how, in Texas, "repeated litigation compensated for the lack of a comprehensive reform coalition" (235). He also suggests that court outcomes play a role in creating political pressure. That is, in line with Scheingold's argument that "judicial rights declarations were like 'bargaining chips'" (235), Bosworth suggests that there is some political interdependence between the public and the branches of government that should be part of any account of education finance reform policy.

In this chapter, we answer the question of whether policy change will occur through the legislature or through the courts. We do so by integrating two areas of scholarship so we can begin to understand the question of why reform happened in some states, but not in others, and in those states with education finance reform, why it was court ordered in some states, while in others the legislature enacted education finance reform. We argue that this is critical to understanding the outcome of reform efforts since finance reform outcomes are likely to differ depending on whether the reform is through the legislature or through the courts. To understand and predict this change, we characterize the state policy environment as consisting of political, legal, and strategic factors that would lead to policy change by the courts or by the legislature. We find that a combination of political and strategic factors influences legislatures and the courts, but that law matters greatly to the courts, particularly state constitutional education clauses. We also find that institutional structure influences the degree to which politics matters to the courts.

CHAPTER 3: CITATION PATTERNS IN EDUCATION FINANCE POLICY

Certain state court decisions, and by extension, the state courts themselves, are more influential than other decisions and other state courts. While the decisions of state supreme courts are final within their jurisdictions, state high courts often look to the decisions of other courts for guidance. They sometimes also retrospectively cite the decisions of other courts in order to justify their actions. We explore what the causal factors are that lead a state supreme court decision to cite the decisions of a sister state court. In addition we examine the factors that lead to the citation of specific decisions of other state courts.

Chapter 4: When Citations Are Not Enough

While the preceding chapter focuses on the influence of state courts as measured by citations, this chapter acts as a bridge between our focus on citation patterns in chapter 3 and our examination of policy diffusion of education finance reform through the courts. We lay out why citations and citation patterns are inadequate to explain and understand why some courts adopted education finance reform and why other courts did not.

Chapter 5: Policy Diffusion through Courts

The diffusion literature has shown that states learn and emulate similarly situated states that have previously adopted the policy under consideration. Much of this research has been conducted among legislatures, showing that national or state legislatures often look to other nations and states for leadership in a particular policy domain. In this book, we apply the concept of diffusion to state courts. We examine when courts choose to follow the actions of other courts, even though they may fail to cite those courts in their final decision. We do so through the examination of court-ordered state education finance reform and its three waves of education finance reform. Using a dyadic dataset from 1974 until 2010, we find that state courts do emulate other state courts but that emulation is different from legislative emulation and different for each wave of reform.

Chapter 6: Conclusion—How State Courts Move and Change Policy

In our concluding chapter we summarize our findings and offer both suggestions for future empirical research for the scholarly community as well as our normative views on how to remedy school financing and how litigants, courts, legislatures, and executives ought to approach future cases dealing with this pivotal issue.

Chapter 2

Why Courts?

Introduction: Politics, Law, and Education Finance Reform

In a democratic system of governance, we expect policy adoption and policy change to come through the legislative branch of government. We know, however, that policy change can come through the courts, albeit within the legal set we construct in chapter 1. In the United States, court-mandated policy change occurs at both the federal and state levels. In this chapter, we examine the state political environment behind education finance reform. We answer the question of why policy change occurs through courts as opposed to legislative reform.

To understand and predict this change, we characterize the state policy environment as consisting of political, legal, and strategic factors that would lead to policy change by the courts or by the legislature. We find that a combination of political and strategic factors influences legislatures and the courts, but that law matters greatly to the courts, particularly state constitutional education clauses. We also find that institutional structure influences the degree to which politics matters to the courts.

While much literature on courts and policy change examines the federal courts in such areas as abortion (e.g., Hull and Hoffer 2001), racial discrimination (e.g., Kluger 1975), and environmental policy (e.g., Melnick 1983), state courts and their policy impact have had much less examination. This is curious because state legislatures write far more state legislation than the United States Congress writes federal law. Most legal work and legal practice is done at the state level. The police power of states, the power that allows the states to enact laws for the health, safety, and welfare of its residents, gives state legislatures wide latitude to write law over a wide

Parts of this chapter are drawn from Roch and Howard (2008).

variety of permissible areas. Congress with its constitutional limitations has less freedom to legislate over such a wide scope.

Because of this many policy domains are left to the states, including such areas as marriage and divorce and, perhaps most prominently, as we reviewed in chapter 1, education. While scholars have created an extensive literature examining policy changes within states, much of this literature focuses largely either on policy change as coming through either the state legislatures or through the state courts with little attempt to incorporate the interaction of state courts and state legislatures. This literature also does not account for current scholarship on state court decision making or examine how courts and legislatures interact in the policy-making process, and how each particular branch can either defer or encourage the other branch to take the lead in making public policy.

Literature on state courts shows that their decisions are a function of attitudes or policy preferences, constrained by institutional considerations, as well as constraints from the separation of powers system inherent in each state (Hall 1992; Brace and Hall 1990, 1995; Hall and Brace 1999; Langer 2002). Much of this literature assumes that decisions reached by state courts of last resort are largely independent of other state courts of last resort. Each state court has its own preferences, laws, particular set of institutional constraints, and it confronts different governors, publics, and state legislatures in rendering decisions. In addition, legal factors such as precedent within the state, state legislative history, and state constitutional and statutory language also play a role.

Research on state policy change often characterizes the policy environment as consisting of internal and external factors, such as public ideology and policy adoption in neighboring states. However, the policy-making environment is a bit more complex. While this framework is broad enough to encompass and allow for the influence of changing information and institutional structure on legislative policy, the models created from this framework fail to account for the fact that in many policy domains those seeking to change policy often resort to courts, and not the legislature, and even then, change sometimes fails to occur through either branch of government. Nor does it account for the interactive nature of the policy environment where legislatures sometimes prefer that courts enact policy change, or where courts continually have to prod legislatures to follow through on court-mandated policy rulings.

In this chapter, we try to answer the question of why education finance reform change occurs through the courts as opposed to the legislature, and why courts sometimes have to produce multiple rulings in a policy domain. As noted in chapter 1, education finance reform has been largely left to the states in the aftermath of *San Antonio Independent School District v. Rodriguez* (1973), the Supreme Court decision that held that there is no federal constitutional right to equalized school financing. This issue is critically important because democratic theory suggests and empirical research shows that courts and legislatures can have significantly different influences on the outcome of the policy change and, in particular, education finance reform (Manwaring and Sheffrin 1997; Murray, Evans, and Schwab 1998; Wood and Theobald 2003).

By integrating these two areas of scholarship we can begin to understand the question of why reform happened in some states but not in others, and in those states with education finance reform, why it was court ordered in some states, while in others the legislature enacted education finance reform. To understand and predict this change, we characterize the state policy environment as consisting of political, legal, and strategic factors that would lead to policy change by the courts or by the legislature. We examine each in turn.

The Political Environment

We first consider the role of the political environment, a key component of most studies of state-level policy change. Scholars have long agreed that, to a great extent, public preferences may influence policy change (Kingdon 1989; Verba and Nie 1972; McClosky and Zaller 1984; Wlezien 2004). As Kingdon notes, "It is likely that the constituency imposes some meaningful constraints on Congressmen's voting behavior" (1989, 68). The influence of public preferences also has been demonstrated in a range of studies examining policy change in the states. For instance, Hill and Leighley (1992) demonstrate a link between the cultural conservatism of a state's citizens and state welfare payments. Meier and McFarlane (1992) show that abortion funding within a state is a function of the relative liberalism of a state's congressional delegation, while Wood and Theobald (2003) demonstrate the link between the conservatism of a state's citizens and state revenue allocations to school districts (these allocations are also a function of the actions of both court and legislative action).

More recent scholarship continues to find this pattern of responsiveness. For example, using several decades of data, Caughey and Warshaw find that the more liberal the public is in a particular state, the more liberal, over time, will be the state policy. The authors find that this change is gradual and takes several years to occur (2018).

A state's broader cultural orientation may also influence policy change and the methods chosen to initiate policy change. For instance, Elazar (1966, 1994) characterizes states as having predominantly one of three different cultural orientations: traditional, individualistic, and moral. According to this characterization, traditional states are less likely to adopt policy innovations and their general orientation is largely conservative; for example, Fisher and Pratt (2006) find that more traditional states are more likely to use the death penalty. In individualistic states, limited government involvement is favored and policy change is more likely to be driven by particular interests, and in moral states, a strong public interest orientation should support broad-based reform for the public good. For example, Koven and Mausolff (2002) find that more moral states have higher expenditures on education when compared to more traditional states, and Mead (2004) finds that moral states are most likely to have successful welfare reform. Thus, a moral orientation should similarly support a greater likelihood of education finance reform.

However, we should also expect moral states to have a greater likelihood of reform through the legislature as opposed to the courts. A more moral state should have a legislature that reflects such values, and thus should be more sympathetic to education finance reform, leading to a greater likelihood of legislative education finance reform. This in turn means that a more moral state should be less likely to have reform through the courts.

Public preferences are not alone in driving institutions to change policy. The extent of the existing problem may also influence the likelihood of policy change. For instance, Berry and Berry (1994) report that states are more likely to adopt a tax increase when a fiscal crisis exists within the state. Wood and Theobald (2003) demonstrate that state courts are more likely to mandate education finance reform when there is greater inequality in the financing of a state's schools. The degree of partisan conflict, for example, gridlock, between houses in the state legislature may limit the likelihood of change even when there exists significant inequality in education finance across schools. While gridlock might not stop policy change, it can have an inhibiting impact (Krehbiel 1996).

Policy adoption by the states may also vary as a function of the resources available to the state. Hill and Leighley (1992) demonstrate that states with higher per capita incomes also have higher welfare expenditures per capita. In the case of education finance, the income capacity of a particular state should help determine the availability of state funds to aid less well-off districts. Thus, wealth should influence prospective decision making since the availability of such funds may increase the certainty of the future success of such reform.

Neighboring state reform should also help assess the impact of a proposed policy by providing an existing laboratory to study the effect of policy change (Walker 1969; Gray 1973; Berry and Berry 1990). According to Walker (1969), by learning about the impact of policies in other states, policy-makers may increase their ability to predict the potential impact of policies in their own state. Mooney (2001) further suggests that such diffusion is most likely during the early stages of a policy's implementation and in cases when policies are likely to have geographically based impacts.

Of course, particularly for education finance reform, other state characteristics also influence the political environment. For example, much of the debate on education finance reform often pits well-to-do school districts against poorer districts. As the number of poorer districts increases, the demand for education finance reform should increase and so should the probability of education finance reform.

In addition, interest groups may influence policy change and, in particular, many such groups seek to influence the ongoing debate over education reform. Perhaps no interest group has a greater interest in the outcome of education finance reform than teachers' unions. As some scholars have noted, teachers' unions are often seen as opposing any and all types of education reform (Boyd, Plank, and Sykes 2000). One paradigm asserts that teachers' unions engage in rent-seeking behavior (Cowen and Strunk 2014), in that the concern of these unions lies in increasing teacher salary and benefits and not in seeking any financial equity for school districts. In part due to their opposition to school vouchers and charter schools, teachers' unions have been marked as reform opponents by their counterparts: for-profit firms that advertise a reduction in cost while maintaining educational quality in part by hiring nonunionized employees (Boyd, Plank, and Sykes 2000, 205).

Of course, the goals of teachers' unions and reformers are not mutually exclusive, and, in fact, both together may offer the most promising road to improving educational outcomes (Johnson and Kardos 2000; Casey 2006). As Ogletree states:

> In all, the growth in state spending on prisons and criminal corrections has outpaced the growth in education spending. However, unlike the push for funding parity between rich school districts

> and poor school districts that occurred during the aftermath of Rodriguez, there does not seem to be a concerted, serious push to reverse the trend of the growth in prison spending outpacing the growth in education spending. (2013, 543)[1]

Even where the goals of unions and reformers coincide, then, because different line items in the education budget represent a zero-sum game, education finance reform and teacher professionalization at times compete for the same resources. Some reforms, in other words, are seen as a threat to income and livelihood to the union membership and are therefore opposed by the union (see, e.g., Moe 2011, 2014).

Law and the legal environment. While courts and legislatures are both embedded in the same larger political environment, their decision context is likely to differ. For instance, past research suggests that electoral constraints cause legislatures to act as prospective decision-makers—they are likely to be concerned with assessing the probabilities of the effect of potential legislation (Krehbiel 1991; Mayhew 1974). Thus, information in the policy environment that increases the legislature's certainty about the relationship between a bill and a set of preferred policy outcomes should increase the likelihood of legislative action.

Courts, on the other hand, are often thought of as badly suited to act as prospective decision-makers, usually possessing neither the electoral authority nor information to realize the impact of their decisions on the future allocation of resources (see Fuller 1960). Moreover, their agenda is reactive as opposed to proactive (Horowitz 1977, 264). Adjudication and lawmaking are very different, with the actors focusing on very different factors. Courts must wait until a lawsuit appears on their docket before they can take any action.[2] Because of this, courts are more likely to act as retrospective decision-makers—they are interested in the realized impact of existing laws (see Rogers 2001, 84), and in ensuring that the prospective decision-makers follow established constitutional rules and boundaries.

There has been significant research on the use of courts to bring about policy change (Rosenberg 2008; Howard and Steigerwalt 2011). Much of this literature shows how interest groups use the courts to achieve policy objectives. Initially, scholars posited that disadvantaged groups used the courts to achieve goals denied through the political process (Cortner 1968; Olson 1990). Later research, however, showed that interest groups on all sides of the political spectrum resorted to the courts. Advantaged as well as disadvantaged groups sued to attain policy goals to supplement, enforce, or maintain legislative gains. For example, business interests and conservative interest groups as well as traditionally liberal and politically disadvantaged groups have used the courts either by participating as parties to the litigation or through filing of amicus briefs (Caldeira and Wright 1988; Unah 2003). As Unah (2003, 66) noted, pursuing rights in court is not something that is restricted to disadvantaged groups. Individuals and groups have goals and the decision to go to court is consistent with obtaining these goals. In support of this calculation, scholars have theorized and found evidence to support the concept that litigants act rationally when deciding to proceed to trial or even appeal a decision to United States Supreme Court (Bebchuk 1984; Songer, Cameron, and Segal 1995).

The retrospective nature of adjudication implies that the stronger the law is to change existing school finance, the greater the likelihood of the court ordering reform, all else equal. For instance, the content of state constitutions varies considerably, often incorporating different language to articulate the legal rights of its citizens or extending overt protections that the US Constitution does not. One prominent example is that of constitutional provisions and education. Most state constitutions have provisions guaranteeing free public education. While many of these only speak of the obligation to provide free education, several states have much more detailed provisions describing the funding of, or providing for, uniform or efficient free public schools.[3] These legal provisions should act as a lens through which litigants and judges assess the degree of inequality within a state and decide whether equalities are in fact great enough to justify reform through the courts. In general, the greater the existing problem, the greater should be the likelihood that a court will order reform.

However, perceptions of inequalities may also be influenced by other factors. Several decades of scholarship have shown that court decisions are not premised solely on law, legal or adjudication factors. Court decisions are a function, to a significant degree, of policy preferences of the judges (Segal and Spaeth 1993). State high court decisions are also a function of state judicial policy preferences (Hall 1992; Kilwein and Brisbin 1997). However, not all state high courts have the same freedom to impose personal policy preferences. The institutional environments of courts show significant state-level variation. Unlike the federal system, in which judges once nominated and confirmed have lifetime tenure, the states have differing selection and retention methods. Scholarship shows that the selection and retention processes also are determinants of outcomes (Brace and Hall 1990; Hall 1992; Canes-Wrones, Clark, and Kelly 2014), and that elected judges often act as representatives of the electorate. For instance, research has shown responsiveness of state courts to public opinion in the area of sentencing (Kuklinski and Stanga 1979), and retaliation by the public in the form of recall voting when judicial votes were inconsistent with public attitudes on the death penalty (Culver and Wold 1986). Other research demonstrates that competitive judicial elections are just as contested as elections in the House of Representatives (Hall 2001).

In addition, despite fears that elections provide little real accountability, elected judges do appear to alter their behavior in response to a perceived risk of electoral reprisal (Hall 2001; Huber and Gordon 2004; Canes-Wrones, Clark, and Kelly 2014). In addition, research by Langer (2002) demonstrates how the relative autonomy of state high courts affects their ability to pursue policy objectives—more autonomous courts were more likely to premise rulings on personal preferences while elected courts are more likely to follow the wishes of the electorate. Thus, while law and legal issues matter far more to judges than to elected legislative officeholders, elected judges should show a greater deference and more sensitivity to political factors than appointed judges.

Finally, the strength of prominent interest groups should also impact the likelihood of court-ordered reform by both elected and appointed judges. Interest group involvement is not limited to seeking legislative change. Interest groups use the courts to achieve policy goals (Cortner 1968). Although early research focused on disadvantaged groups' use of the courts and theorized that such groups used the courts because they were not able to access the political system otherwise, later research discounted this "disadvantaged group" theory by showing that even powerful interest groups use the courts to achieve policy objectives (Olson 1990; Unah 2003). Interest groups can set the agenda for courts and influence legal change. Evidence exists that interest groups through the use of court briefs have influenced judicial decision-making (Caldeira and Wright 1988; O'Connor and Epstein 1983). Thus, the strength of teachers' unions should lead to a lower probability of court-ordered reform.

The strategic calculations of state-level actors. For the past few decades, scholars have increasingly relied on SOP models to study the relationship between a changing policy environment, institutional structure, and actions of courts and legislatures (see, e.g., Ferejohn and Shipan 1990; Westerland 2017). These positive political theorists argue that courts frequently must move policy toward legislative preferences in order to prevent overrides that would lead to less desirable policy outcomes. Justices must be mindful of political constraints (Epstein and Knight 1998). Although SOP models at the federal level examine potential constraints imposed by the legislature, in the case of state courts, institutional structure creates political constraints that may influence how courts are likely to perceive subsequent strategic interaction. For example, while liberal state high courts may prefer to equalize education finance spending, depending upon institutional structure there is the potential for retaliation. This threat would be the most pronounced when the judges are elected and least likely when courts are appointed. Courts will be the most willing to adjudicate when the court is appointed and thus free from retaliation and the most reluctant to adjudicate when there is divergence from public preference and the court is elected.

Legislatures also make strategic calculations. Rogers (2001, 88) argues that legislatures will prefer to have the courts repeal laws due to the high transaction costs associated with legislative repeal and the information asymmetry between courts and legislatures (a product in part of their decision-making contexts). If the legislature, however, believes that the policy preferences of the court differ from their own, then they must consider that potential action through the courts may restrict their future ability to achieve their preferred policy goals. In this case, a prospective legislature may act to circumvent action by the court.

Thus, legislatures in states with strong constitutional provisions might want the court to take action so as to avoid unpopular legislation. Legislatures should also attempt to preclude court action in cases when they suspect that future court action may hinder the ability of the legislature to achieve its own policy goals. For example, this might be more likely when judges are appointed and thus not as accountable to the political system. From the preceding, we now present our hypotheses.

Hypotheses

Predicting the actions of state legislatures. As we have discussed, we expect that legislatures will be influenced by political and prospective factors and by strategic considerations. Since remedying disparities in education is a liberal position, we expect that reform should be more likely in more liberal states (McIver, Erikson, and Wright 1993; Berry et al. 1998). As prospective actors, legislatures should be more likely to enact reform in cases when states have greater resources and when there is increasing evidence of successful reform in neighboring states (Walker 1969; Gray 1973). We expect that reform is unlikely to occur when there is legislative conflict. Due to transaction costs, legislatures may prefer to allow the courts to enact reforms, especially when there are stronger educational provisions in the state's constitution; however, in cases when the courts are less constrained, such as when judges are appointed, the legislatures may act to circumvent the courts:

H1a. Legislative-ordered education finance reform will be more likely in more liberal states.

H1b. Legislative-ordered education reform will be more likely in more moral states, and less likely in states with an individualistic culture.

H2a. Legislative-ordered education finance reform should be more likely in a state when neighboring states have experienced education finance reform.

H2b. Legislative-ordered education finance reform will be more likely in wealthier states.

H3a. Legislative-ordered education finance reform will be more likely in states with appointed judges.

H3b. Legislative-ordered education finance reform will be less likely in states with strong education provisions.

H4. Legislative-ordered education finance reform will be less likely in states with legislative conflict.

Predicting the actions of state courts. As we have discussed, we expect that reform will be more likely in those states that have very detailed constitutional provisions providing for uniform or efficient free public schools. Institutional structure, however, should also determine the direction of the state courts. In particular, when courts are appointed rather than elected we expect that retrospective factors should influence the likelihood of court action, whereas political and other institutional factors should greatly influence the likelihood of reform for elected courts. Thus, we expect that the extent of inequality in financing will be more likely to influence reform in states where judges are appointed. When courts are elected, more liberal policy preferences among citizens should increase the likelihood of reform through the courts. Institutional structure should also influence how courts view potential strategic interaction. For instance, when appointed, more liberal judges should also be more likely to enact reform, given the decreased threat of potential retaliation:

H1. Court-ordered education finance reform should be more likely in states that have constitutional provisions guaranteeing uniform and efficient education.

H2. Court-ordered education finance reform would be more likely in states in which there exists greater disparity in education financing and state judges are appointed.

H3. Court-ordered education finance reform should be more likely in states in which citizens are more liberal and state judges are elected.

H4. Court-ordered education finance reform should be more likely in states in which the state court is more liberal and judges are appointed.

H5. Court-ordered reform will be more likely in states with a more individualistic and less moralistic culture.

Data

To examine the likelihood of legislative or court reform empirically we gathered state-level data from 1974 through 2010. We start with 1974 because that is one year after the United States' Supreme Court decision in *San Antonio Independent School District v. Rodriguez* (1973), the decision that effectively ended any federal constitutional right to equal funding.

We use the coefficient of variation in instructional expenditures to measure the extent of education financing inequality in a given state. For the years 1980 to 1994, the coefficient of variation was obtained from tables made available by the NCES (Hussar and Sonnenberg 2000). Coefficients for 1974 to 1979 were calculated using data on instructional expenditures made available through the ELSEGIS Survey of Local Government Finances—School Systems, and coefficients for 1994 to 2010 were calculated using the NCES Local Education Agency (School District) Finance Survey (F-33) Data. Values for the coefficient of variation were interpolated for the years 1976, 1979, 1984, and 1985. We used per capita income as a measure of state wealth, and thus as the measure of the capacity to correct education resource inequality.

To capture the influence of reforms in neighboring states, we created two variables. The first reflects whether a neighboring state has enacted legislative reform, and the second reflects whether a neighboring state has experienced court-ordered reform. By legislative reform we mean whether or not the legislature has enacted legislation that seeks to amend or change the formula for funding public schools that increases funding for poorer school districts. For court-ordered reform, we coded a "1" if the state court sided with the plaintiffs against the state, locality, or district and increased funding for the poorer school districts. We eliminated Hawaii from the analyses since Hawaii has a unified education system, as well as Alaska since we are not able to measure the influence of neighboring state reform.

For state ideology we use revised citizen and governmental liberalism scores. These scores have been revised using data provided by Klarner (2003) and updated through 2010 based on the methodology described in by Berry et al. (1998). These measures consider changes in ideology over time and thus may have an advantage over other measures—including those developed by Erikson, Wright, and McIver (1989; McIver, Erikson, and Wright 1993; Wright, Erikson, and McIver 1985). The citizen liberalism scores are based on the congressional roll call voting scores of House incumbents and estimated scores for challengers; these scores are then weighted by the percentage of the vote received in the general election. The governmental liberalism scores are based on the aggregated scores of the estimated ideology of the two chambers of the state legislature and the ideology of the governor. In addition, the benefit of using these state ideology scores is that they are strictly comparable to measures of state-level judicial ideology developed by Brace, Langer, and Hall (2000), which we use for the measures of judicial state ideology. Because of this, we can directly compare the influence of public and governmental ideology and judicial ideology on finance reform.[4]

We also include indicators representing Elazar's (1966) classification of the US states into three political-culture types. We include a variable that takes on a value of 1 when states are individualistic and a variable that takes on a value of 1 when states are classified as traditional. This specification allows us to compare the likelihood of reform in either individualistic or traditional states to those classified as moral, which is our baseline.

We also include other measures of state characteristics that would lead to education finance reform. First we gathered information on urbanization from census data in order to gauge the number of urban school districts;

this variable is measured as a percentage of the state's population living in areas defined as urban by the census.[5] In addition, in order to capture further the degree of potential inequality, we also included measures of income inequality using data from the World Inequality Database developed by economists Pikkety and Zucman. This measure provides the percentage of fiscal income held by the top 10 percent of the population for each state over time. Our measure of state legislative conflict is based on annual data provided by Klarner (2003), which we updated through 2007 using data on his website, and for the years 2008 to 2010 the data were obtained from the National Conference of State Legislatures. The variable takes on a value of 0 when the same party controls both houses of the legislature, a value of .5 when control is split in either house, and a value of 1 when a different party controls each house. For interest groups we include a measure of the strength of teachers' unions. This variable takes on a value of 0 if the union does not have the power to strike and the employer has no duty to negotiate with the union, a 1 if the employer has a duty to negotiate, and a 2 if unions have both the right to strike and the employer has a duty to negotiate (Freeman and Valletta 1988).

To assess the varying legal environments across states, we examined state constitutions and state judicial ideology. For each state constitution, we coded the state as a 1 if the state constitution contained a clause providing for a right to a free public education, and a 2 if the section or clause contained specific language on funding or provided for a uniform or efficient funding system. As previously stated, we use aggregated measures of judicial state ideology developed by Brace, Langer, and Hall (2000).

We include the same variables across each of our models for the sake of uniformity, with one important difference. Since a key determinant of our model of court outcomes is judicial structure, we include and interact two dummy variables to capture the role of court selection procedures in directing the attention of judicial actors. One indicates whether judges are subject to elections, coded as 1, if yes, 0, otherwise, and the second indicates whether judges of the high court are nominated (1, if yes, 0, otherwise). This leaves judges who are appointed and then subject to retention elections as the baseline. We include these dummy variables in our legislative reform model, and, since we theorize that judicial structure will determine outcomes, we then create dummy variables with the coefficient of variation, citizen ideology, and judicial ideology in our court reform model through an interaction with these variables.

Models, Methodology, and Results

We test our expectations about when legislatures act to change policy by constructing a model that takes on the following form:

Legislative Reform = β_0 + β_1 Political Information + β_2 Strategic Considerations + β_3 Controls + ε

We test our hypotheses about the probability of education finance reform through the state courts by estimating the following model:

Court-ordered Reform = β_0 + β_1 Legal Information + β_2 Political Information + β_3 State Judicial Institutional Structure + β_4 Strategic Considerations + β_5 Controls + ε

Thus, first we model the likelihood that the event of legislative reform will occur during a given year, while our next analysis models the likelihood that the event of court reform will occur during a given year. In these models, our dependent variables take on two values: a value of 0 when there has been no reform, and a value of 1 when there has been reform. In our legislative model, state years are included in the data set until legislative reform occurs in a particular state. States without legislative reform are included for all years. In our courts model, states enter the dataset once litigation occurs and remain in the dataset even once court reform occurs due to the threat of subsequent litigation. For both models we rely on a logit estimation procedure and report robust standard errors, clustered on states, to control for the potential influence of any outlying observations (Western 1995). In addition, to control for maturation effects, we include in the model spline variables for different sets of years (see Beck, Katz, and Tucker 1998). We use these rather than time point dummies, because of the existence of a number of years in which no reform occurred, and for the sake of efficiency, since with our numerous variables we were concerned with our degrees of freedom.

We present the results of our analyses in tables 2.1 and 2.3 and omit the splines since they do not add any substantive interpretation to our analyses. To aid in the interpretation of the coefficients, we also present the average marginal effects of observing reform that occurs as the values of each of our independent variables change in tables 2.2 and 2.4.

Table 2.1. Logistic Regression Results for Legislative Reform

Variable	**Legislative Reform**
Coefficient of Variation	7.503* (3.760)
Citizen Liberalism	0.101 (1.753)
Per Capita Income (in $1,000)	0.042 (0.089)
Proportion Urban	–0.911 (1.472)
Teachers' Unions	–1.414* (0.540)
Income Inequality	0.075 (7.796)
Governmental Liberalism	–0.433 (1.396)
Individualistic	–1.931* (0.817)
Traditional	–1.064 (0.783)
Legislative Conflict	0.180 (0.581)
Neighboring Court-Ordered Reform	0.538 (0.461)
Neighboring Legislative Reform	0.241 (0.726)
Constitutional Provision	–0.111 (0.421)
Elected Judges	0.660 (0.525)
Appointed Judges	2.049* (0.629)
Constant	481.329 (370.558)
Observations	902

Chi2 = 82.19***, Pseudo R2 = .11, * = $p < .05$, ** = $p < .01$, *** = $p < .001$ (two-tailed test).

Table 2.2. Average Marginal Effects for Legislative Reform

Variable	Average Marginal Effect
Coefficient of Variation	0.245
Citizen Liberalism	0.003
Per Capita Income (in $1,000)	0.001
Proportion Urban	–0.030
Teachers' Unions	–0.046
Income Inequality	0.002
Governmental Liberalism	–0.014
Individualistic	–0.063
Traditional	–0.035
Legislative Conflict	0.006
Neighboring Court-Ordered Reform	0.018
Neighboring Legislative Reform	0.008
Constitutional Provision	–0.004
Elected Judges	0.022
Appointed Judges	0.067
Constant	
Observations	902

We provide average marginal effects that provide the change in probability of reform for a 1-unit change in each variable while all other variables are held constant at their values. The base probability = 0.04.

Turning first to legislative action, as we hypothesized, and confirming many traditional explanations of legislative behavior, our results indicate that legislatures do respond to the need for education finance reform depending upon the significance or size of the problem, the electorate, and interest group pressure. The greater the variation in district finances, the greater the likelihood that the legislature will intervene. The average marginal effect is 24.5 percent as a state changes from one in which there is little variation in educational spending to one with large variations—this is a substantial increase of the baseline probability, when all independent variables are set to their mean, of 3.5 percent. Conversely, a powerful teachers' union will decrease the probability of reform. Figure 2.1 shows that unions have the greatest marginal effects on legislative reform when state laws provide unions the right to strike and employers have a duty to negotiate. Culture also appears to impact the process. As hypothesized, a moral state is more likely to enact reform. Thus, while education finance reform is an important issue that has the potential to impact hot button topics, including the

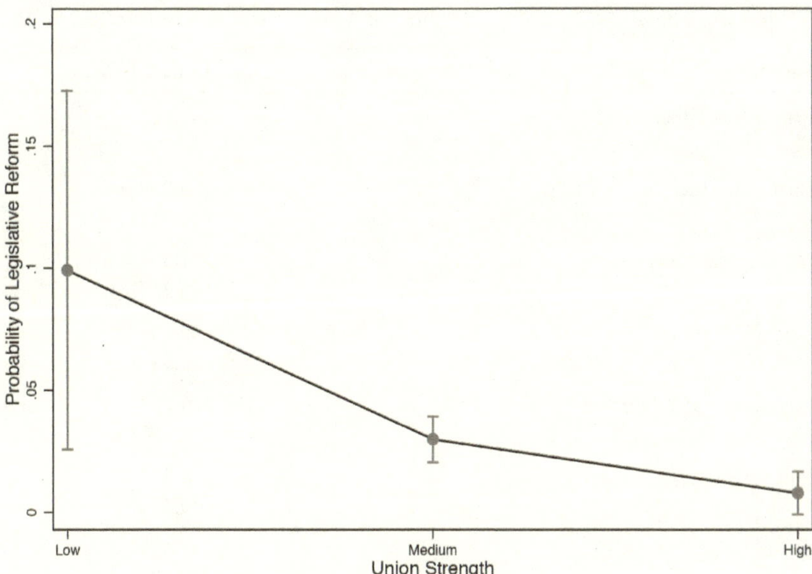

Figure 2.1. The Effect of Union Strength on Legislative Reform (Predicted Probabilities with 95% CI).

quality of education and real estate values, these results show legislatures respond in a rational manner to external demands. Somewhat surprisingly, citizen preferences did not influence the probability of legislative reform. It is possible, however, that citizen preferences are captured by the existing education inequality measure, and by measures of political culture.

However, we also show that legislatures are aware of the political environment and respond strategically to the other branches of government. We find that an appointed judiciary matters to the legislature. We work on the assumption that a legislature would calculate that an appointed judiciary would have a greater probability of intervening in this matter and rule on education finance reform. This in turn would mean that the legislature would lose much control of the process. In figure 2.2 on page 52, we see that when states have appointed judges, the average marginal effect for legislative reform is 13.5 percentage points, an increase more than three times larger than the base probability of 3.5 percent.

The story behind court-ordered reform is a bit more complex and depends in larger measure on institutional structure, which in turn implies a degree of strategic thinking on the part of the judges. Thus, while legislators sometimes might prefer that courts deal with such a difficult and potentially

Table 2.3. Logistic Regression Results for Court-Ordered Reform

Variable	Court-Ordered Reform
Proportion Urban	–1.167 (0.754)
Per Capita Income (in $1,000)	0.050 (0.058)
Income Inequality	1.409 (5.223)
Teachers' Unions	–0.127 (0.347)
Governmental Liberalism	–0.733 (0.871)
Individualistic	0.672 (0.474)
Traditional	–0.137 (0.679)
Legislative Conflict	–0.330 (0.473)
Neighboring Legislative Reform	–0.132 (0.510)
Neighboring Court-Ordered Reform	–0.180 (0.395)
Constitutional Provision	0.786* (0.404)
Elected Judges	–2.766 (1.791)
Appointed Judges	–4.419* (2.078)
Judicial Liberalism	–0.325 (1.157)
Citizen Liberalism	–1.956 (1.704)
Elected* Judicial Liberalism	–0.728 (1.575)
Appointed Judges* Judicial Liberalism	–2.001 (1.800)

Variable	Court-Ordered Reform
Coefficient of Variation	–9.048 (5.777)
Elected* Coefficient of Variation	9.254 (7.123)
Appointed Judges* Coefficient of Variation	26.354* (9.724)
Elected* Citizen Liberalism	3.042+ (1.732)
Appointed Judges* Citizen Liberalism	2.997 (2.435)
Constant	–1.348 (2.180)
Observations	1232

Chi2 = 325.37***, Pseudo R2 = .112, * = p <. 05, ** = p < .01, *** = p < .001 (two-tailed test).

Table 2.4. Average Marginal Effects for Court-Ordered Reform

Variable	Average Marginal Effect
Proportion Urban	–0.053
Per Capita Income (in $1,000)	0.002
Income Inequality	0.063
Teachers' Unions	–0.006
Governmental Liberalism	–0.033
Individualistic	0.030
Traditional	–0.006
Legislative Conflict	–0.015
Neighboring Legislative Reform	–0.006
Neighboring Court-Ordered Reform	–0.008
Constitutional Provision	0.035
Observations	1232

We provide average marginal effects that provide the change in probability of reform for a 1-unit change in each variable while all other variables are held constant at their values. The base probability = 0.05.

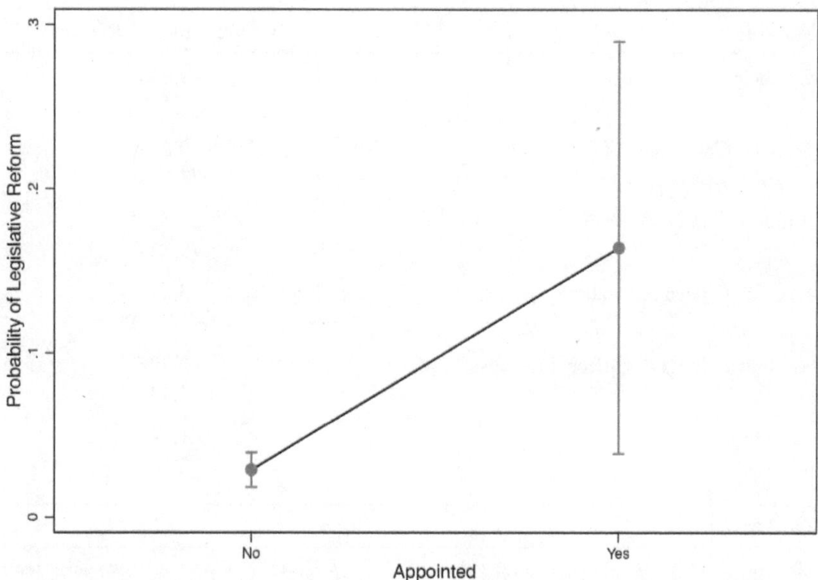

Figure 2.2. The Effect of Appointed State Judges on Legislative Reform (Predicted Probabilities with 95% CI).

politically troubling issue, that presupposes that the court-ordered reform will be similar to the policy preferences of the legislature, and that courts react to the same influences and pressures as legislatures.

An independent, appointed court might have preferences different from that of the legislature since the electorate to which in theory the legislature must respond has no control over the judiciary. Thus, an appointed judiciary might lead a legislature to conclude that they would best deal with the matter directly, as it suggested by our results in table 2.2. Then, as numerous studies show, law does matter to courts (Corley, Steigerwalt, and Ward 2013; Bailey and Maltzman 2011). By 2010, twenty-eight state high court challenges to the constitutionality of public school financing had succeeded to the extent that courts ordered some type of reform.

When we examine our empirical model for court reform, we see that it performs well. The base probability is 5 percent. The results show that law and institutional judicial structure are critical in calculating the likelihood of court-ordered reform as well as politics and state culture. Thus, the institutional design of the court strongly influences the court's attention within the state policy environment. However, it is not just the institutional design of appointed or elected judges that influences court-ordered reform, but also the interactions of these features with critical political and strategic state factors that are critical to determining the role of the courts.

Importantly, law matters in this area, independent of judicial preference. The strength of constitutional provisions guaranteeing a free education can increase the probability of court-ordered reform. We show in the second column of table 2.3 that as the constitutional provisions variables changes from 1 to 2 (from less strict amendments to those that are more strict, containing specific language on funding) the average marginal effect is 3.5 percentage points. With a baseline probability of 5 percent, a strong constitutional provision then increases the probability of court-ordered reform, all else being equal, to close to a 9 percent chance of occurring.

In contrast, judicial preference does not seem to matter for either appointed or elected judges. This finding is in contrast to significant research on the federal and state level regarding voting and judicial attitudes, and it may reflect the singular nature of education finance reform and the strength of state constitutions in this policy area.

Much depends on institutional structure, which affects the degree of influence of inequality in instructional expenditures. We illustrate this relationship in figure 2.3. We see that appointed judges are most likely to order

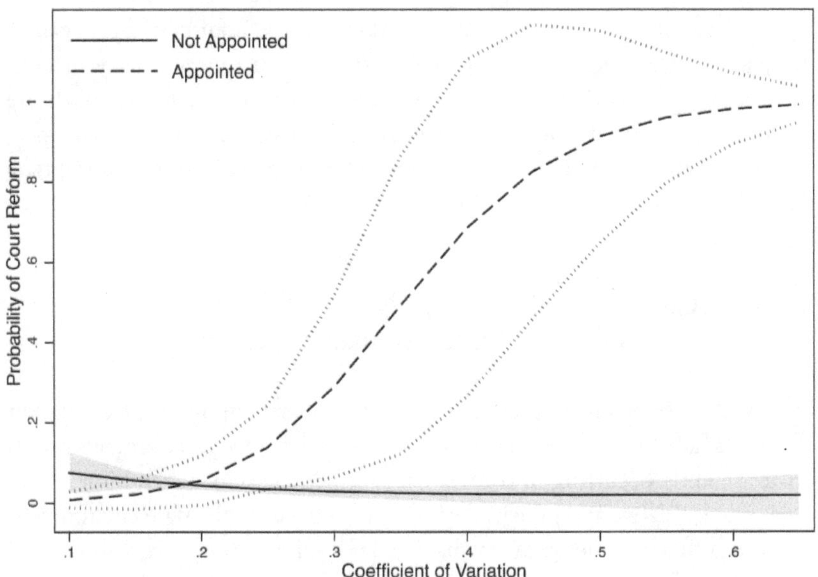

Figure 2.3. The Effect of Judicial Appointment and Inequality in Funding on Court Mandated Reform (Predicted Probabilities with 95% CI).

reform when confronted with the retrospective factor of greater inequality. As the inequality in funding increases, appointed judges become increasingly likely to enact reform. In contrast, changes in the inequality of funding in a state appear to have little influence on the behavior of judges who face a retention election. This finding is consistent with more than two decades' worth of literature that shows judges facing reelection do alter votes to align with constituent preferences (Hall 1992; Huber and Gordon 2004). It also shows how the median justice on courts with retention elections will move left or right within his or her indifferent set depending upon the particular set of constraints each judge or court confronts. It also presents evidence that the set of policy options that a court can offer is itself constrained.

This impact of the inequality in financing is substantively greater than in the case of legislative reform. Thus, if the problem is acute, an appointed court has the freedom to address the issue and this occurs independent of policy preference or court liberalism. Interestingly, we do find that elected courts will follow the policy preferences of the electorate. Thus, our findings show that elected courts and those subject to retention elections face substantially different sets of constraints than appointed courts.

Putting several of these probabilities together shows that if there is a state with significant variation in education expenditure, an appointed high court, and a strong constitutional educational provision, there is a high probability of court-ordered education finance reform. Despite claims by many activist judiciaries and unelected judges acting as policy-makers, the evidence shows that in the area of education finance reform, courts are acting in a preferred normative manner. They use the law and retrospective information, regardless of policy preference, to fashion an appropriate judicial remedy.

Conclusion: Predicting the Institutional Agent of Court-Ordered Finance Reform

In this chapter, we have sought to provide understanding and explanation of why education reform occurs in courts and legislatures, and why it is predominantly occurring in courts. We consider the strategic and interactive process of legislative and judicial decision-making within the state environment and the differences between lawmaking and adjudication. Legislatures and courts are different and react to different state factors, although the more a court's institutional court structure resembles the structure of a legislature, that is, if the court is elected, the less clear the distinctions are between them.

However, simply put, the legislature defers to the court on education finance reform when the court is elected, and thus presumably shares the same policy preferences. Elected courts are more numerous than appointed courts. However, that is not the entire story. An appointed court will be more likely to intervene in education finance the greater the variation in educational expenditure throughout the state, the clearer the constitutional framework. Given these conditions, and the strategic deference of the legislature, it is thus not surprising that we have seen much more court-ordered finance reform than legislative reform.

Admittedly, we lack the information about the initiation of legislation necessary to model the selection process driving the consideration of legislation. As a consequence, we are also not able to limit our analysis of legislative reform to those years in which legislation was in fact being considered.

We next turn to our attention to the courts. First we focus on citations. It is not sufficient for a court to order education finance reform. A court needs to justify its actions in the opinion. Citations are often thought the key to justification of the reasoning behind the court opinion. Specifically, we examine the factors that lead to the citation of specific decisions of other state court.

Chapter 3

Citation Patterns in Education Finance Policy

Introduction

As we have shown in chapter 2, courts play a major role in the implementation of education finance reform. This is partially because state legislatures are sometimes unable or unwilling to act. In the last chapter we note courts often produce reform orders that substantively differ from those issued by legislatures. This is because state supreme courts have more than a policy interest in the outcome of education finance reform cases; as legal actors, state supreme courts have an institutional and professional fidelity to the law in addition to their policy preferences.

As we note in the previous chapters, education finance is a complex issue raising legal dilemmas in which a given state supreme court likely has little adjudication experience. In these instances, the typical source of legal guidance, a state's case law, will give little direction on the proper course of action, the court may have limited resources to research the matter, and the wording of the state constitution may be vague.

Facing a dearth of information, state supreme courts likely look to trusted sources for guidance. Frequently, these trusted sources are peer courts that have previously adjudicated education finance cases. Turning to outside sources confers prestige on the cited court, which enables the cited court to become a network leader exerting influence well beyond the geographical boundaries of its jurisdiction. However, just as there are variations between state legislatures, there are differences between state supreme courts that

---

Parts of this chapter are drawn from Gleason and Howard (2015).

include the volume of cases heard, the professionalism of the court, and the strength of the state constitution. The net result is that some state supreme courts occupy a prestigious place in the education finance network, whereas others are more marginal. This is important because a more prestigious court is one that is more attractive to peers in other states. Its reputation thus serves as a heuristic in the search for citations. Accordingly, then, a court with high prestige is more likely to be cited and thus more likely to have an impact on the shape of case law beyond its jurisdictional boundaries.

Case law forms the basis of legal decisions. This is intuitive as seeking out previous case law on education finance allows state supreme courts to cite the decisions of peer courts. Having case law to cite, even if from another jurisdiction, helps state supreme courts root their decisions in the law. This ensures that the actors charged with carrying out the decision view the court's reasoning as legitimate and rooted in the state constitution rather than an expression of partisan preferences. While this would be true of a state supreme court decision in any issue area, it arguably takes on a more important dimension in politically charged issue areas such as education finance where the audience is presumably broader than in a more obscure issue area. Beyond questions of legitimacy, drawing on the use of the legal reasoning provided by other courts also has a practical element to it; drawing on previously established case law saves state supreme courts from the work associated with developing and justifying a new legal standard. Particularly, as there is remarkable variation in the resources state supreme courts have at their disposal (Squire 2008), using legal frameworks developed by another court is a remarkably attractive option. While precedent and citations are a mainstay of the legal profession, it is important to differentiate the two forms they take: vertical and horizontal citations.

Vertical Citations and the Power of Precedent

Vertical citations are the default that often comes to mind when thinking about citations. They are inclusive of a court citing its own precedent or citing the decisions of a superior court. Failure to cite relevant vertical precedent is notable. It would, for instance, be quite odd for the Fourth Circuit to decide a case dealing with prayer in schools without reference to *Lee v. Weissman*[1] or for the US Supreme Court to decide a case about student speech without reference to *Morse v. Frederick*.[2]

In the first example the Fourth Circuit is inferior to the US Supreme Court and thus bound by its precedent. In the latter example, the norm of stare decisis dictates a given court follow its own previous decisions as precedent. While not every decision is bound to become an important precedent that is cited in every subsequent case (Fowler and Jeon 2008), vertical citations are properly thought of as "required." To return to our examination of education finance reform, state supreme courts are bound by their previous education finance decisions. To illustrate this point, consider the South Carolina Supreme Court's decision in *Abbeville County School District v. State*.[3] It would be exceptionally odd for any South Carolina court, state supreme court or otherwise, to decide an education finance case without reference to *Abbeville*. In this instance, the South Carolina courts have a guiding precedent in *Abbeville* that can help adjudicate future education finance cases. However, not all jurisdictions are as fortunate as South Carolina to have vertical precedent to shape their future education finance decisions. In many jurisdictions there is a lack of precedent on the topic of education finance. Indeed seven state supreme courts have never adjudicated a case on education finance. Should one of those states decide an education finance case, its case law likely offers little to no guidance.

Of course, having previous decisions dealing with education finance is no guarantee previous case law will provide guidance as a new case may pose a vexing problem that cannot be solved with existing precedent.[4] This problem is compounded as many states have only adjudicated a handful of education finance cases and their precedents may offer only limited guidance. While this problem could arise in virtually any issue area, it is particularly pronounced in education finance because the US Supreme Court has vacated the field, leaving state supreme courts as the effective last word on education finance reform with no federal guidance. In these instances, state supreme courts often turn to horizontal citations.

Horizontal Citations and Persuasiveness

Unlike vertical citations, horizontal citations are discretionary and never required. Horizontal citations are made between sister courts—in our case, between two different state supreme courts. For instance, the Idaho Supreme Court citing the Georgia Supreme Court in one of its decisions would be an instance of a horizontal citation. Of course, the choice of the

Georgia Supreme Court over, for example, the Ohio Supreme Court is left entirely to the discretion of the citing court and no legal norm or threat of higher review compels a state supreme court to utilize a particular (or any) horizontal citation. Thus, the decision to give a horizontal citation to a particular court conveys a measure of prestige (Mott 1936; Caldeira 1985). Aside from the professional accolades to a peer court for helping guide a court, horizontal citations also have important consequences as the reach of the cited opinion can now extend beyond the jurisdictional boundaries of the citing court.

From a practical perspective, horizontal citations are intuitive. It does not make sense to "reinvent the wheel" if another court has already developed a framework for adjudicating complex education finance cases. In this way, state supreme courts save the resources that would normally be expended crafting an opinion in a hereunto unexplored area of law while also justifying their decision in previous case law. Yet, for all their utility, horizontal citations also raise normative concerns; courts that are in no way accountable to voters or political elites in the citing court are able to shape the contours of case law in that state. To return to our previous example of South Carolina's *Abbeville* decision, should another court cite that decision, the reach of the South Carolina Supreme Court's decision extends past the geographical boundaries of the state. For these reasons, scholars repeatedly return to the topic of horizontal citations at both state supreme courts and the federal courts of appeals over the past eighty years.

The first studies of horizontal citations occur in 1936 when Mott notes that the prestige in which state supreme courts are held varies from court to court. That is to say, those courts that are well regarded by their peers are most likely to receive citations and become "leaders" in shaping state case law on a national level. Decades later this finding gains additional support from Merryman (1954), who finds that the California Supreme Court draws more extensively on the decisions of some courts over others. In a series of articles Caldeira (1983, 1985, 1988) delves into the predictors of judicial reputation, which he terms "prestige." He finds judicial reputation is largely the product of social diversity, judicial professionalism, political ideology, and case load. That is to say, courts that have diverse populations are most likely to deal with novel legal questions that result in opinions which are valuable to peer courts (1983). Later, Caldeira (1985) turns to the question of transmission of precedent between courts and finds the characteristics of the cited court predict citations between courts, as well as the cultural and regional linkages between courts. Later work notes that there are distinct patterns in terms of which courts frequently transmit citations between each other (Caldeira 1988). Among the court-level characteristics, Caldeira (1985) notes that a specialized case load increases citations. For instance, given its jurisdiction encompasses Wall Street, the New York Court of Appeals is a leader in securities law. Likewise, the California Supreme Court has emerged as a leader in criminal procedure case law to the point that the US Supreme Court has relied on its expertise in crafting its decisions. The net result is more cases, and by proxy more diverse cases, allowing courts to develop a reputation that leads peer courts to turn to them when facing a particularly vexing problem in the cited court's area of expertise. This is intuitive, because a more extensive body of case law should produce more opinions, at least some of which should be attractive to peer courts.

While Caldeira's work is instrumental to our understanding of horizontal citations, the time frame of the study is an important limit in any contemporary analysis. Caldeira uses data from the 1970s and much has changed in the ways state supreme courts operate over the past several decades. Many courts have become more professional by, for instance, obtaining an intermediate court of appeals. The rise of intermediate courts of appeals has afforded state supreme courts more discretionary control over their dockets, which allows courts to spend more time researching opinions and, by proxy, presumably including more horizontal citations. Perhaps, though, the greatest change in the way state supreme courts operate is the ease with which they can access information. The advent of digital legal research tools such as Lexis and Westlaw makes searching for out-of-state opinions much easier and presumably should increase the frequency of horizontal citations between peer courts.

Recently, Hinkle and Nelson (2016) revisited Caldeira's (1985) study using data from 2010. Remarkably, though state supreme courts and society in general have gone through a sea change in professionalism and technology, the predictors of coalition formation remain largely unchanged. Accordingly, the line of research beginning with Mott (1936) provides a robust framework for understanding horizontal citations. Still, there are reasons to suspect the predictors of prestige and citation may not directly port to education finance decisions. Education finance, as we have argued, is a special issue area not only because of its profound impact on American society, but also because state supreme courts are very often the final word on this topic.

Since the US Supreme Court's decision in *Rodriguez* to vacate the issue area, state supreme courts do not have the threat of higher judicial review in education finance cases and may accordingly decide differently than in issue areas where higher review is possible. There is some support for this expectation in work by Gleason and Howard (2015), who examine the factors that predict citation pair formation between state supreme courts in education finance cases. They note that in the broader citation pair formation literature, Comparato and Gleason (2013) note more ideologically distant courts are more likely to form citation pairs, perhaps in an effort to stave off US Supreme Court review. However, they find that in the second wave, state supreme courts are more likely to form citation pairs with each other when the courts are ideologically close to each other. Gleason and Howard (2015) continue that this is likely because education finance has no threat of higher review.

Thus, without the threat of higher court review, state supreme courts may very well alter their behavior from what is seen in horizontal citations more generally. This indicates the adage about states as the "nation's laboratories"[5] is particularly true in education finance. Importantly, this suggests that the experiences and legal reasoning of one state is of value to other states (see, e.g., Volden 2006). To continue the analogy, state supreme courts are able to write the definitive conclusion for the laboratory report, often by drawing on the expertise of their peers in other states. It is possible for a small number of states to become leaders and thus a template for other state supreme courts dealing with education finance nationwide (e.g., Caldeira 1988).

While previous work establishes which courts are prominent in the state supreme court citation network writ large (Mott 1936; Caldeira 1983, 1985) and other work explores citation pairs in the education finance network (Gleason and Howard 2015), no work explores what makes a court prestigious in the education finance citation network.

Hypotheses: State Supreme Courts Shaping Education Finance Reform

We accordingly now turn to an examination of which state supreme courts are best situated to shape education finance reform opinions in both the second and third waves. The states that are prominent in this network can shed light on the development of education finance policy, which depends to a great extent on court actions, but also on the spread of policy through courts, more generally. In general, we seek to do several things with our analysis. First, from a purely descriptive point of view, we seek to determine which state supreme courts are most prestigious in the education finance citation network. Second, we explore what makes state supreme courts more prestigious. In the latter we draw upon previous work on both state supreme court citations broadly and education finance more specifically.

It is an axiom that the more experience one has with a given task, the better one will become at performing that task. This is certainly true of the state supreme court citation network. Caldeira (1985) notes that the courts with the most case law are horizontally cited the most frequently, if only because there is more case law to ultimately cite. Importantly, Caldeira (1985) also notes that specialized case law leads to more citations as well. Those states with higher rates of urbanization and higher GDPs are more likely to be cited as their unique litigation environment will likely result in them dealing with novel legal questions well before their peers (see also Hinkle and Nelson 2016). Extended to the education finance network, it follows:

H1. State Supreme Courts with more previous education finance decisions are more likely to be prestigious.

There is remarkable variation in terms of state supreme court resources and the provision of resources has important consequences for the output of the court (Squire 2008). Caldeira (1985) notes that those courts with the most resources receive the most citations presumably because they are more meticulously developed. In their update, Hinkle and Nelson (2016) find much the same; more professional courts are more likely to receive citations. Given that the courts with the most resources will be best able to produce opinions that are attractive to other courts, accordingly, we expect:

H2. State Supreme Courts that are more professional are more likely to be prestigious.

Finally, it is important to recall that state supreme courts are legal institutions as well as political institutions. Some states have more detailed language in their state constitutions on education finance. To illustrate this point, consider that the Kansas Constitution (art. 6, sec. 1) speaks only of "establishing and maintaining public schools." However, the Idaho Constitution (art. 9, sec. 1) calls for a "general, uniform and thorough system of public, free, common schools." Differences in state constitutional provisions have shown differences in the diffusion of policy from both state legislatures and state supreme courts (Roch and Howard 2008; Gleason and Howard 2015). Accordingly, we expect:

> **H3**. State Supreme Courts with stronger education finance state constitutional provisions are more likely to be prestigious.

Data and Methods

In order to explore horizontal citations between state supreme courts we utilize social network analysis. Social network analysis is an ideal way to observe interactions between actors since this method is premised on the idea that observations are interdependent (Wasserman and Faust 1994). That is to say, the actions of a given state supreme court are shaped by the actions of the other courts. In our case, this is a prudent choice as prestige is shaped not only by the actions of a given court, but also by the way in which other courts respond to its decisions. These interdependencies generate a network, which is typically depicted with the familiar "spiderweb" plots, called sociograms. Additionally, social network analysis generates underlying statistics, such as density and centrality, which give a more precise way to evaluate the shape of a network. In our particular instance, we will be able to use both the sociograms and the underlying network statistics to test our hypotheses. We now proceed in several parts. First, we briefly overview the social network analysis data and methods we employ. Subsequently, we examine citation patterns in both the second and third waves of the education finance network.

Social network analysis is focused on edges (otherwise known as ties) between nodes. A node is an actor. For instance, in a friendship network a node would be an individual and in a cosponsorship network a node is a senator (Fowler 2006). In our case, a node is a state supreme court. Some nodes are connected by edges. What constitutes an edge varies depending on the study. In a friendship network an edge is likely a measure of whether two people are friends, and in a cosponsorship network an edge is whether two senators cosponsor a bill together. Graphically, they are depicted as lines connecting nodes. Ultimately, the edge is the unit of analysis in any social network model. In our case, a citation edge occurs when a given state cites the education finance decisions of another state supreme court in its decisions (Gleason and Howard 2015).[6] Fortunately, we are able to draw upon Gleason and Howard's (2015) data. However, as social network data is somewhat unintuitive, we now turn to an explanation of how data is transformed into a format amenable to social network analysis.

Any data used in a social network application must be in network format. In this case that means the data must be presented in a fifty by fifty matrix where each possible pair of courts is represented once. Each of the fifty columns represent one state supreme court. Likewise, each of the fifty rows represent one state supreme court each. If, for instance, we were interested in how frequently Idaho cites Illinois, we would only need to look to the intersection for each of those two states.[7] This matrix is then transformed into a network object using the statnet package in R (Handcock et al. 2012). We now turn to an illustrative example to demonstrate how this process works.

Consider the following example. Assume there are three state supreme courts: A, B, and C. Court A cites Court B, but not Court C. Court B cites only Court C and Court C cites neither of its peers. We take this data and construct a social network matrix that lists the three courts both vertically and horizontally. We insert a value of 1 (denoting an edge) in the proper intersection (e.g., A:B is set to 1 as Court A cites Court B, while C:B is set to 0 as Court C does not cite Court B).[8] The resulting matrices are then transformed into networks. Via statnet, we then generate several useful data to evaluate the network ranging from the graphical depictions in sociograms, network-level statistics, and node-level metrics. We briefly overview these tools.

Table 3.1. Social Network Matrix Example

	Court A	**Court B**	**Court C**
Court A	–	1	0
Court B	0	–	1
Court C	0	0	–

Perhaps the most well-known social network tool is the sociogram. Sociograms can be thought of in terms of a core and a periphery. Actors near the core, or center, of the network are central actors that are typically well connected and exert a great deal of influence. In our context, being in the core means a given court is cited and cites widely. Conversely, actors on the edge of the network, or the periphery, are more marginal and do not participate in the network extensively. They may cite only a handful of other states. They, accordingly, exercise less influence in the overall network. Finally, other actors completely abstain from the network and do not cite at all. These actors are termed "isolates" (Wasserman and Faust 1994). In order to facilitate easy interpretation of our sociograms, we do not display our isolates.[9]

While sociograms are a useful tool to evaluate networks, it is also useful to look at the underlying statistics that generate the network to gain a more fine-tuned understanding of how the network is structured. These statistics can be thought of as the underlying mathematical explanation for why the sociogram is structured as it is. This can be done at both the network and node levels. At the network level, one of the most useful metrics is density. Density is a measure of the proportion of potential edges that are actually formed (Kadushin 2012). This statistic ranges from 0 in a network where no edges are formed to 1 in a network where all potential edges are formed. In our case, lower density means less citation is occurring and higher density means more frequent citation. At the node, or court, level centrality is perhaps the most useful statistic. Centrality is a broad class of measures that account for how centrally located a given actor is in a network. There are a number of centrality measures, such as betweenness, closeness, eigenvector, and prestige. Each of these measures focuses on a different aspect of centrality, which may or may not be relevant in a given study depending on the theoretical context (Friedkin 1993; Neal 2014).[10] In our case, the most useful form of centrality is prestige centrality. Prestige centrality measures how well regarded a given actor is by other actors in the network. An actor with high prestige centrality is regarded as a network leader by other actors. This measure is generated by taking the total number of citations each state supreme court receives and scaling the measure in relation to one another (Wasserman and Faust 1994). Here, prestige becomes our primary variable of interest.

We also generate a number of measures to test our hypotheses. We denote number of previous cases with a count of the total number of education finance cases decided in each wave. We draw this measure from Roch and Howard (2008) and update it accordingly. We denote the professionalism of each state supreme court with the professionalism scores developed by Squire (2008). This measure is advantageous because it creates a single composite score for professionalism for each court by combining a number of predictors, such as discretionary control of the docket, the number of law clerks, judicial pay, and the presence of an intermediate court of appeals. Finally, we note the strength of state constitutional provisions with the measure developed by Roch and Howard (2008). This measure ranges from 0 for states with weak education provisions in their constitutions to 2 for states with extensive education finance constitutional provisions.

Results

Collectively, our analysis provides insight into the education finance citation network. Our findings collectively indicate that some courts are more prestigious in the network than others, suggesting their relative significance in influencing the legal reasoning within the network of education finance reform. We note some differences between waves, further highlighting that the issue area is dynamic. However, none of our proposed predictors for prestigious courts hold. This suggests that either the citation network is driven by some more complex process, or that citations are in and of themselves not the best way to evaluate prestige.

The sociograms for both the second and third waves are displayed in figure 3.1. The top panel displays the second wave and the bottom displays the third wave. Looking first to the second wave, the density is 0.13. This means 13 percent of all possible edges between courts are formed. However, these edges are not randomly distributed. Some courts are more likely to be connected than others. This is immediately clear when evaluating the sociogram graphically. The New York Court of Appeals along with the Colorado Supreme Court are centrally positioned in the network core in the second wave. The core is rounded out by a number of other courts that ring the core. Several other state supreme courts exist on the periphery and connect with only one or a handful of other state supreme courts.

While much of the work on horizontal citations writ large stresses citations patterns are consistent over time (Caldeira 1985; Hinkle and Nelson 2016; Merryman 1954), we note differences between the second and third waves of the state supreme court education finance citation network. In the third wave, displayed in the bottom panel of figure 3.1, the core is more

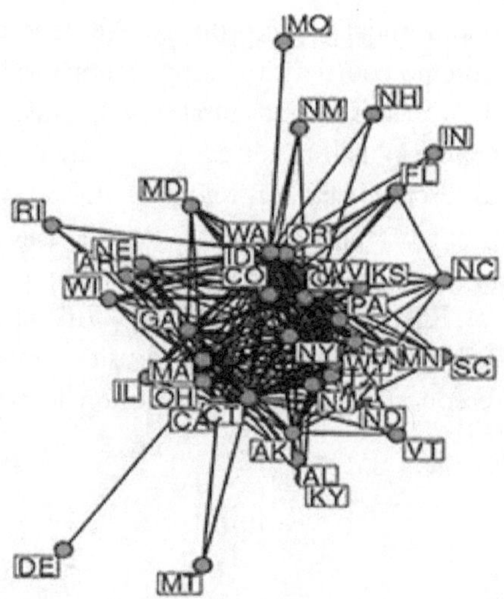

Wave 2 Citation Network

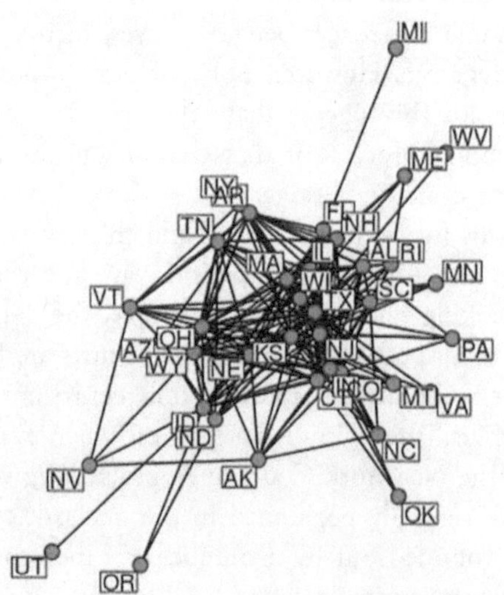

Wave 3 Citation Network

Figure 3.1. Wave 2 and Wave 3 Citation Networks.

densely populated than in the second wave. New York and Colorado, the most prestigious courts in the second wave, exist on the edge of the core. There are several small clusters of states within the core. This perhaps suggests that small clusters of state supreme courts group together. In this wave, the periphery is altogether smaller, suggesting states are more connected and work together in the core of the network. This collectively provides support for Gleason and Howard's (2015) assertion that education finance networks are different than the citation network writ large, where prestigious courts from one era are typically still prestigious in the next. Accordingly, what makes a court prestigious in the second wave may be altogether differ from makes a court prestigious in the third wave.

While sociograms are useful, they only tell part of the story. It is also worthwhile to look at node (court) level network statistics. Table 3.2 lists state supreme courts ordered by prestige for each wave. In the second wave the most prestigious court is Tennessee, though it is closely followed by several courts. This suggests that there are several leaders in this network. However in the third wave, Connecticut is the most prominent court and does not have many close peers in terms of prestige. This indicates that Connecticut largely occupies the most prestigious place in the network by itself. To illustrate how the network can evolve and change with time, Tennessee falls to twenty-first place in the third wave. At this point we have established that there are differences from one wave to the next in terms of prestige. We now turn to an attempt to explain why these differences manifest.

With the shape of the network and its most prestigious actors defined, we turn to evaluating our hypotheses. Recall, we expect that those courts with the most previous education finance decisions will be the most likely to receive citations. Table 3.3 displays the state supreme courts and their prestige ordered by the number of cases each court adjudicates in each wave. We note that West Virginia has the most cases in the second wave. While our hypotheses suggest this should propel West Virginia to a prestigious place in the network, it is ranked nineteenth in overall prestige. Shifting our focus to the third wave, we note New Jersey has the most cases with six. However, in terms of overall prestige it is in ninth place. As noted in table 3.2, the most prestigious third wave court is Connecticut; yet it has two total cases in the wave, which places it in eleventh place for overall volume. This suggests prestige in the citation network is the product of something other than the number of education finance cases each has adjudicated, such as perhaps the quality of the resulting opinions.

Table 3.2. Citation Prestige

Second Wave			Third Wave		
Rank	**Court**	**Prestige**	**Rank**	**Court**	**Prestige**
1	TN	0.058	1	CT	0.09
2	AZ	0.055	2	IN	0.082
3	NJ	0.055	3	CO	0.077
4	TX	0.055	4	TX	0.064
5	WY	0.055	5	NE	0.06
6	KS	0.047	6	AR	0.056
7	ND	0.044	7	WY	0.047
8	IL	0.04	8	IL	0.043
9	NY	0.04	9	NJ	0.039
10	AR	0.036	10	NY	0.034
11	CT	0.036	11	ND	0.03
12	MA	0.036	12	MA	0.03
13	NE	0.036	13	AL	0.03
14	OK	0.033	14	SC	0.026
15	WI	0.033	15	OH	0.026
16	CO	0.029	16	KS	0.026
17	MD	0.029	17	AZ	0.026
18	MN	0.029	18	NH	0.021
19	WV	0.029	19	WI	0.017
20	PA	0.025	20	VT	0.017
21	AL	0.018	21	TN	0.017
22	FL	0.018	22	NV	0.017
23	GA	0.018	23	MN	0.017
24	KY	0.018	24	ID	0.017
25	OH	0.018	25	PA	0.013
26	VT	0.018	26	NC	0.013
27	NC	0.011	27	MT	0.013
28	NM	0.011	28	ME	0.013
29	RI	0.011	29	FL	0.013
30	AK	0.007	30	RI	0.009
31	ID	0.007	31	WV	0.004
32	IN	0.007	32	VA	0.004
33	MT	0.007	33	UT	0.004
34	NH	0.007	34	MI	0.004
35	OR	0.007			
36	DE	0.004			
37	MO	0.004			
38	SC	0.004			
39	WA	0.004			

Table 3.3. Case Count and Prestige

Second Wave Citation Network				Third Wave Citation Network			
Rank	Court	Case Count	Prestige	Rank	Court	Case Count	Prestige
1	WV	3	0.029	1	NJ	6	0.039
2	NY	2	0.040	2	TX	5	0.064
3	CT	2	0.036	3	NH	5	0.021
4	WA	2	0.004	4	AZ	4	0.026
5	CA	2	0.000	5	IL	3	0.043
6	AZ	1	0.055	6	NY	3	0.034
7	NJ	1	0.055	7	AL	3	0.030
8	WY	1	0.055	8	OH	3	0.026
9	KS	1	0.047	9	ID	3	0.017
10	AR	1	0.036	10	TN	3	0.017
11	OK	1	0.033	11	CT	2	0.090
12	MD	1	0.029	12	NE	2	0.060
13	PA	1	0.025	13	AR	2	0.056
14	GA	1	0.018	14	WY	2	0.047
15	OH	1	0.018	15	MA	2	0.030
16	AK	1	0.007	16	KS	2	0.026
17	ID	1	0.007	17	MT	2	0.013
18	MT	1	0.007	18	PA	2	0.013
19	OR	1	0.007	19	AK	2	0.000
20	SC	1	0.004	20	OR	2	0.000
21	MI	1	0.000	21	ND	1	0.030
22	TN	0	0.058	22	SC	1	0.026
23	TX	0	0.055	23	MN	1	0.017
24	ND	0	0.044	24	VT	1	0.017
25	IL	0	0.040	25	WI	1	0.017
26	MA	0	0.036	26	FL	1	0.013
27	NE	0	0.036	27	ME	1	0.013
28	WI	0	0.033	28	NC	1	0.013
29	CO	0	0.029	29	RI	1	0.009
30	MN	0	0.029	30	MI	1	0.004
31	AL	0	0.018	31	VA	1	0.004
32	FL	0	0.018	32	CA	1	0.000
33	KY	0	0.018	33	KY	1	0.000
34	VT	0	0.018	34	LA	1	0.000
35	NC	0	0.011	35	MD	1	0.000
36	NM	0	0.011	36	MO	1	0.000
37	RI	0	0.011	37	OK	1	0.000
38	IN	0	0.007	38	IN	0	0.082
39	NH	0	0.007	39	CO	0	0.077

continued on next page

Table 3.3. Continued

Second Wave Citation Network				Third Wave Citation Network			
Rank	Court	Case Count	Prestige	Rank	Court	Case Count	Prestige
40	DE	0	0.004	40	NV	0	0.017
41	MO	0	0.004	41	UT	0	0.004
42	HI	0	0.000	42	WV	0	0.004
43	IA	0	0.000	43	DE	0	0.000
44	LA	0	0.000	44	GA	0	0.000
45	ME	0	0.000	45	HI	0	0.000
46	MS	0	0.000	46	IA	0	0.000
47	NV	0	0.000	47	MS	0	0.000
48	SD	0	0.000	48	NM	0	0.000
49	UT	0	0.000	49	SD	0	0.000
50	VA	0	0.000	50	WA	0	0.000

Our next hypothesis holds more professional courts are more likely to receive citations. Recall, we would expect that courts with more resources are in a better position to write opinions that are attractive to other state supreme courts and are thus more likely to be prestigious and be centrally located in the network. Across multiple studies, courts with more prestige are more likely to receive citations. While prestige has historically been measured in a number of ways, such as the evaluations of law professors (Mott 1936), state population, or GDP (Caldeira 1985), more recent work creates an index of a number of prestige predictors such as judicial salary, law clerk support, discretionary control of the docket, and the presence of an intermediate appellate court among other predictors (Squire 2008). We utilize this more recent composite measure to create table 3.4, which ranks all state supreme courts in order of their prestige scores. We note that our two most prominent courts in both waves (Tennessee and Connecticut) are not among the most prestigious courts in the network.[11] Much like our case volume hypothesis, the most prestigious courts are not the most professional courts. The most professional court, California, has a prestige score of 0 in the third wave. This is most likely attributable to the fact that the California Supreme Court did not decide any education finance cases in the third wave. This suggests then that professionalism does not predict prestige in the citation network for either the second or third waves.

Table 3.4. Professionalism in the Citation Network

Rank	Court	Professionalism	Prestige Wave 2	Prestige Wave 3
1	CA	1.051	0.000	0.000
2	PA	1.007	0.013	0.013
3	MI	0.901	0.004	0.004
4	SC	0.828	0.026	0.026
5	FL	0.828	0.013	0.013
6	NY	0.818	0.034	0.034
7	WV	0.813	0.004	0.004
8	NJ	0.807	0.039	0.039
9	IL	0.803	0.043	0.043
10	LA	0.760	0.000	0.000
11	VA	0.731	0.004	0.004
12	WA	0.724	0.000	0.000
13	DE	0.711	0.000	0.000
14	OH	0.698	0.026	0.026
15	TX	0.694	0.064	0.064
16	NH	0.694	0.021	0.021
17	TN	0.676	0.017	0.017
18	CO	0.671	0.077	0.077
19	AZ	0.669	0.026	0.026
20	GA	0.660	0.000	0.000
21	NC	0.654	0.013	0.013
22	NM	0.650	0.000	0.000
23	MA	0.648	0.030	0.030
24	NE	0.641	0.060	0.060
25	IN	0.638	0.082	0.082
26	MD	0.631	0.000	0.000
27	WI	0.629	0.017	0.017
28	MN	0.627	0.017	0.017
29	CT	0.620	0.090	0.090
30	MO	0.598	0.000	0.000
31	KY	0.593	0.000	0.000
32	AR	0.583	0.056	0.056
33	AK	0.580	0.000	0.000
34	KS	0.574	0.026	0.026
35	OR	0.546	0.000	0.000
36	RI	0.518	0.009	0.009
37	IA	0.458	0.000	0.000
38	AL	0.451	0.030	0.030
39	OK	0.441	0.000	0.000
40	MS	0.438	0.000	0.000
41	ID	0.436	0.017	0.017
42	ME	0.436	0.013	0.013

continued on next page

Table 3.4. Continued.

Rank	Court	Professionalism	Prestige Wave 2	Prestige Wave 3
43	NV	0.407	0.017	0.017
44	MT	0.401	0.013	0.013
45	HI	0.394	0.000	0.000
46	WY	0.347	0.047	0.047
47	UT	0.320	0.004	0.004
48	SD	0.304	0.000	0.000
49	VT	0.297	0.017	0.017
50	ND	0.267	0.030	0.030

Our final hypothesis holds that states with more complex education finance provisions in their state constitutions are more likely to be cited, as those states will pay close attention to education finance cases and may write more exhaustive opinions that will be attractive to other courts. In this instance, as we see in table 3.5, we do find Connecticut is virtually tied for first place. However, it is important to note that the education finance provision only takes on values from 0 to 2, so there is not a great deal of variation in the measure. Tennessee, by contrast, is quite far down the list in thirty-fifth place. This provides qualified support for our contention that states with more extensive education finance provisions in their constitutions will be more prestigious.

Table 3.5. Constitutional Education Provisions

Rank	Court	Education Provisions	Prestige Wave 2	Prestige Wave 3
1	CT	2	0.09	0.09
2	IN	2	0.08	0.08
3	TX	2	0.06	0.06
4	AR	2	0.06	0.06
5	WY	2	0.05	0.05
6	IL	2	0.04	0.04
7	NJ	2	0.04	0.04
8	AL	2	0.03	0.03
9	ND	2	0.03	0.03
10	AZ	2	0.03	0.03
11	OH	2	0.03	0.03
12	NH	2	0.02	0.02

Rank	Court	Education Provisions	Prestige Wave 2	Prestige Wave 3
13	ID	2	0.02	0.02
14	MN	2	0.02	0.02
15	WI	2	0.02	0.02
16	MT	2	0.01	0.01
17	NC	2	0.01	0.01
18	PA	2	0.01	0.01
19	VA	2	0.00	0.00
20	WV	2	0.00	0.00
21	CA	2	0.00	0.00
22	DE	2	0.00	0.00
23	KY	2	0.00	0.00
24	MD	2	0.00	0.00
25	NM	2	0.00	0.00
26	OR	2	0.00	0.00
27	WA	2	0.00	0.00
28	CO	1	0.08	0.08
29	NE	1	0.06	0.06
30	NY	1	0.03	0.03
31	MA	1	0.03	0.03
32	KS	1	0.03	0.03
33	SC	1	0.03	0.03
34	NV	1	0.02	0.02
35	TN	1	0.02	0.02
36	VT	1	0.02	0.02
37	FL	1	0.01	0.01
38	ME	1	0.01	0.01
39	RI	1	0.01	0.01
40	MI	1	0.00	0.00
41	UT	1	0.00	0.00
42	AK	1	0.00	0.00
43	GA	1	0.00	0.00
44	LA	1	0.00	0.00
45	MO	1	0.00	0.00
46	OK	1	0.00	0.00
47	SD	1	0.00	0.00
48	HI	0	0.00	0.00
49	IA	0	0.00	0.00
50	MS	0	0.00	0.00

Collectively, our results demonstrate that explanations for what drives the state supreme court citation network in education finance network are not as simple as pointing to just one causal factor. There are several possible reasons for this. The first explanation is the one posited by Gleason and Howard (2015). Citations are driven by the interplay of a number of predictors for both the citing *and* cited court. For example, they note more extensive constitutional provisions increase the propensity of a court to cite a peer, but constitutional provisions have no bearing whether a court is cited in the third wave. Thus, descriptive statistics cannot provide an adequate explanation for prestige, and more methodologically rigorous explanations for what drives prestige are required. Yet, rather than go down that path, we think it is important to think about alternative conceptualizations of prestige that do not involve citations. Indeed, a host of literature suggests citations are not the ideal way to examine cross-court influence in the education finance network.

Chapter 4

When Citations Are Not Enough

Introduction

Thus far we have denoted prestige via citations. This approach is prudent since citations are often the metric by which cross-court influence is measured (Caldeira 1983, 1985, 1988; Gleason and Howard 2015; Hinkle and Nelson 2016). However, there are reasons to be skeptical about this theoretical assumption. While citations are a legal norm, the extent to which they are utilized is a function of a number of factors, some of which are idiosyncratic to specific courts. This is well summarized by previous research on state supreme court citations, which notes: "Alaska's Supreme Court relies a good deal more on sister courts than does Virginia's Court of Appeals, which almost never cites anybody but itself" (Caldeira 1983, 88). It is possible then that more restrained courts such as Virginia are reading opinions from outside authorities but simply not utilizing them in their opinions. Alaska, on the other hand, makes liberal use of citations. Accordingly, citations between state supreme courts may not fully capture the role of peer courts in shaping judicial outcomes as influence may be present but not attributed.

Just as citations may be used sparingly, they may also be used too liberally. Concerns over citations are compounded as courts may engage in string citations where a number of decisions are cited with little or no treatment of each case individually. A given citation may receive several paragraphs of detailed discussion, it can be included in a footnote, or it can be "buried" deep in a string citation. Because of this, some scholars argue citations add little beyond the impression of legitimacy and do not actually shape the opinion itself (e.g., Anderson 2011; Cross 2010; Garopa and Ginsburg 2012; Blanes i Vidal and Leaver 2013).[1] Thus, even if a state supreme court choses to cite a particular decision, there is no guarantee that citation is meaningful as the legal norm of citations is not consistent, universal, or binding. In the resulting pattern, some courts are more likely to be cited, but the pattern does not necessarily denote influence on the outcome (Caldeira 1983, 1985, 1988).

Taken collectively, using citations to understand the diffusion of education finance reform decisions through state courts is at best an unreliable measure. At worst, citations lack validity and do not capture what we are interested in observing: how courts factor sister courts' decisions and experiences into their own decision-making process. While precedents can be indicators of decision-making factors, they can just as well be used to justify decisions ad hoc: "Some of these authors bind the judges; others provide convenient make-weights and masks for preconceived views of public policy" (Caldeira 1988, 29; see also Lupu and Fowler 2011; Segal and Spaeth 1993, 2002). Thus, recently scholars have looked beyond citations in order to measure cross-court influence. We follow their lead and rerun our analysis where we examine policy adoption rather than citation.

What Else Matters

Of course, state court opinions do not, as a rule, cite similar characteristics as a reason for adopting court-mandated education finance reform. Nor do they explicitly write or concede that they are emulating the lead of a sister state court. What court opinions do is cite precedent and law. As we saw in the previous chapter, emulation and citation can occur independent of each other.

Legal factors, furthermore, are not the only source of information that can influence a judge's decision, and a state court's incentive to emulate sister courts differs from the incentive to cite them. State courts are not bound by the decisions of other sister state courts. What is more, their emulation of another court's decision may be viewed as a negative. In other words, citing a decision by a nonfederal court outside the state may lessen the legitimacy of the outcome rather than enhance it. As we saw in the previous chapter, the decision to cite a court is in large part dependent on the prestige of the cited court. Courts chose to cite decisions that have the potential to enhance the legitimacy of their decisions, independent of the substantive issue at hand.

At the same time, regardless of how prestigious courts are, how sister state courts solve the same problems is valuable information to the court.

This is particularly true for a policy as pervaded with uncertainty as education finance reform:

> State constitutions provide legislatures, and ultimately courts, virtually no guidance as to what constitutes an adequate education. There is no agreed-upon list of public education goals (is it producing civic-minded democratic citizens, or productive contributors to the economy). There is no standard for the skills, competencies, and knowledge necessary to serve those goals of an adequate education. Finally, even if the legislature and courts were to craft those standards from whole cloth, how do we determine what resources will produce the desired outcomes? And what background characteristics of students ought to be considered in distributing those resources (e.g., linguistic, economic, and/or genetic disadvantages)? (Koski and Hahnel 2008, 48–49)

Even if the legal judgment is based on state law, judges, similar to citizens and lawmakers, will require more than these legal bases to determine outcomes. And they will likely draw on more information than what they choose to reveal in the written decisions. While it may not always be in the court's interest to include nonlegal justifications, political scientists have long established that judges are influenced by their background and their surroundings.[2] Judges do not live in isolation and information on education finance reform in neighboring states and courts can find its way into briefs judges read and news judges consume.

Consider the aftermath of California's *Serrano v. Priest*[3] decision as explained by Brimley and Garfield:

> The decision was widely hailed on all sides. The press, legislative groups, educators at all levels in the administrative hierarchy, and taxpayer organizations were all enthused. Liberal civil rights adherents rejoiced at the apparent triumph of egalitarianism and conservative property owners rejoiced at the apparently impending demise of the local property tax. (2002, 225, quoting Carrington 1973, 162)

To the degree that judges are family members, neighbors, consumers of news, or simply social beings, the information that influences them will go beyond legal factors presented in briefs. In short, the information that judges may use in justifying their opinion and the information that may (consciously or not) determine their decision can differ. Accordingly, the factors that cause a judge to cite a sister court decision may differ from the factors that affect the outcome. We have looked at citations in the previous chapter. Next, we discuss how we can test whether sister state court behavior influences court outcomes. While precedents can be indicators of decision-making factors, they can just as well be used to justify decisions (Caldeira 1988, 29; see also Segal and Spaeth 1993, 2002; Lupu and Fowler 2013).

Moreover, while the citation of precedents is a legal norm, as Caldeira states, each court has different norms about whether, when, and which sister state courts to cite (Caldeira 1983). In other words, legal norms are not consistent, universal, or binding. A sister court that is emulated may be cited—or not. That is particularly true for citation patterns between state supreme courts, since they are not binding to one another.

Testing the Limits of Citations: Data and Methods

We denote a policy adoption edge when a receiver state enacts reform and the sender state has previously enacted court-ordered reform in that wave. To put it another way, once a court has ordered education finance reform all subsequent states that order reform will form an edge with that state. To create this data, we turn to Howard and colleagues' (2017) data on policy adoption between state supreme courts in education finance decisions. Since their data is in dyadic form, we must transform the dyads into relational data of the form we discuss earlier. Once again, this results in a fifty by fifty matrix where the union of a row and column denotes whether a given state has adopted a policy put forth by another state supreme court. We accordingly now return to our earlier hypotheses; however, we now do so through the medium of policy rather than citation.

Results

Figure 4.1 displays the policy network for the second and third waves of education finance reform. The top panel displays the second wave while the bottom panel displays the third wave. Compared to the citation networks displayed in figure 3.1, we note several differences. Beginning with the second wave in the top panel, the first difference is the relative density of the

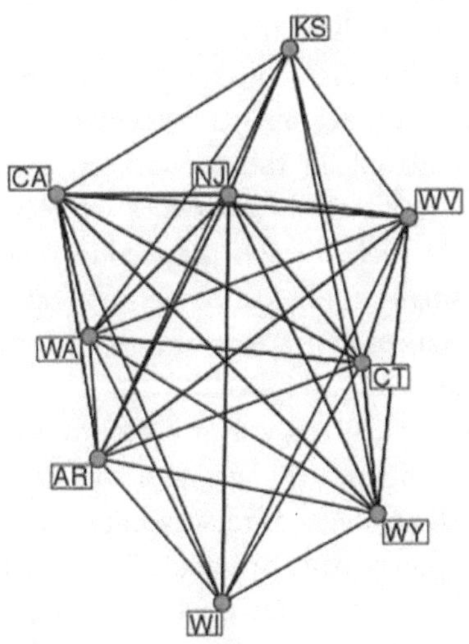

Wave 2 Policy Network

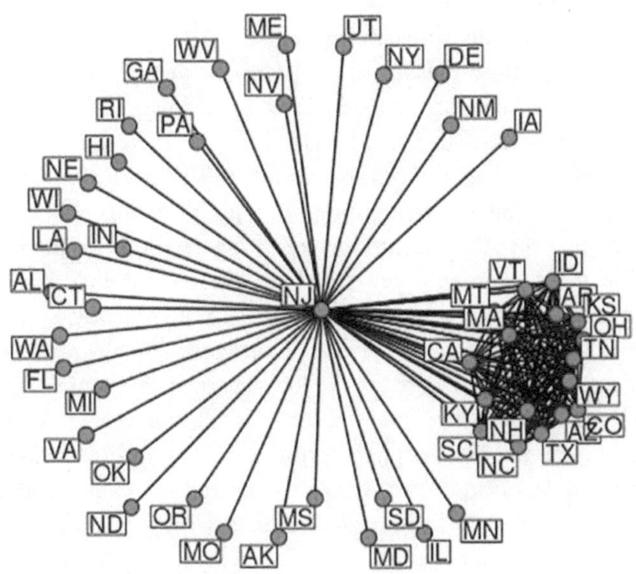

Wave 3 Policy Network

Figure 4.1. Wave 2 and Wave 3 Policy Networks.

network. The policy network is relatively small with only a handful of state supreme courts participating, the density is 0.022 (as opposed to 0.13 for the citation network). This indicates only 2 percent of all possible policy pairs occur. All courts participating in the network are fairly connected to one another, which renders it effectively a network without a periphery (though there are many isolates). This indicates the second wave policy network is a dense clique where a small number of actors interact extensively with each other. This stands in marked contrast to the second wave citation network, which has a distinct core and periphery.

We now turn to a similar analysis of the third wave, which is displayed in the bottom panel of figure 4.1. We note that the third wave network is considerably denser than the second wave network. In the third wave 7 percent of all possible policy pairs are made (as opposed to 9.5 percent in the citation network). In this denser policy network, the core is relatively populated. Unlike the second wave policy network, however, the periphery is well connected to the core via multiple edges. Again, the layout of this network differs considerably from the third wave citation network displayed in figure 4.1. This provides support to the idea that citation and policy are capturing fundamentally different concepts.

Next we examine the descriptive statistics we are able to glean from the education finance policy network. Table 4.1 displays the most prestigious courts in the network. It is immediately clear that there are fewer actors in the policy network than the citation network. This speaks to the concerns that scholars have raised about using citations as a proxy for prestige, as citation prestige may be the product of string citations or negative treatments. The most prominent court in both the second and third waves is New Jersey, which has a prestige score of 0.122. New Jersey is effectively a core unto itself in the third wave policy network. As shown in figure 4.1, it is connected to a dense core on the lower part of the figure where nearly every court is connected to one another. Additionally, New Jersey is also emulated by a number of peripheral actors at the top of the sociogram who do not emulate any other court. Given the central role New Jersey holds in this network, it comes as little surprise that it is easily the most prestigious court in the third wave policy network; the next most prestigious courts lag behind New Jersey considerably (Kentucky and Montana both have prestige scores of 0.087). In both waves New Jersey is the most prominent court. By contrast, in the citation network New Jersey was never the most prominent court, though it did rank third in the second wave citation network and ninth in the third wave citation network.

Table 4.1. Prestige in Policy

Second Wave			Third Wave		
Rank	Court	Prestige	Rank	Court	Prestige
1	NJ	0.151	1	NJ	0.122
2	KS	0.132	2	KY	0.087
3	WI	0.132	3	MT	0.087
4	CA	0.113	4	TX	0.081
5	CT	0.113	5	MA	0.076
6	WA	0.113	6	KS	0.070
7	WV	0.094	7	NH	0.070
8	WY	0.094	8	TN	0.070
9	AR	0.057	9	AZ	0.064
10	AK	0.000	10	WY	0.064
11	AL	0.000	11	NC	0.047
12	AZ	0.000	12	OH	0.047
13	CO	0.000	13	VT	0.047
14	DE	0.000	14	CO	0.023
15	FL	0.000	15	ID	0.023
16	GA	0.000	16	SC	0.023
17	HI	0.000	17	AK	0.000
18	IA	0.000	18	AL	0.000
19	ID	0.000	19	AR	0.000
20	IL	0.000	20	CA	0.000
21	IN	0.000	21	CT	0.000
22	KY	0.000	22	DE	0.000
23	LA	0.000	23	FL	0.000
24	MA	0.000	24	GA	0.000
25	MD	0.000	25	HI	0.000
26	ME	0.000	26	IA	0.000
27	MI	0.000	27	IL	0.000
28	MN	0.000	28	IN	0.000
29	MO	0.000	29	LA	0.000
30	MS	0.000	30	MD	0.000
31	MT	0.000	31	ME	0.000
32	NC	0.000	32	MI	0.000
33	ND	0.000	33	MN	0.000
34	NE	0.000	34	MO	0.000
35	NH	0.000	35	MS	0.000
36	NM	0.000	36	ND	0.000
37	NV	0.000	37	NE	0.000
38	NY	0.000	38	NM	0.000
39	OH	0.000	39	NV	0.000
40	OK	0.000	40	NY	0.000

continued on next page

Table 4.1. Continued.

Second Wave			Third Wave		
Rank	**Court**	**Prestige**	**Rank**	**Court**	**Prestige**
41	OR	0.000	41	OK	0.000
42	PA	0.000	42	OR	0.000
43	RI	0.000	43	PA	0.000
44	SC	0.000	44	RI	0.000
45	SD	0.000	45	SD	0.000
46	TN	0.000	46	UT	0.000
47	TX	0.000	47	VA	0.000
48	UT	0.000	48	WA	0.000
49	VA	0.000	49	WI	0.000
50	VT	0.000	50	WV	0.000

Looking now to how well the number of cases a court has adjudicated that deal with education finance, table 4.2 demonstrates New Jersey deals with the most cases (six) in both waves of the education finance network. Recall, in table 3.5 we note New Jersey is also the most prominent court in the education finance network. This suggests that the number of cases a court adjudicates reflects its prestige in the education finance policy network and provides support for our case-volume hypothesis.

Table 4.2. Case Count and Prestige

Second Wave Policy Network				Third Wave Policy Network			
Rank	**Court**	**Case Count**	**Prestige**	**Rank**	**Court**	**Case Count**	**Prestige**
1	NJ	6	0.151	1	NJ	6	0.122
2	NH	5	0.000	2	TX	5	0.081
3	TX	5	0.000	3	NH	5	0.070
4	AZ	4	0.000	4	AZ	4	0.064
5	AL	3	0.000	5	TN	3	0.070
6	ID	3	0.000	6	OH	3	0.047
7	IL	3	0.000	7	ID	3	0.023
8	NY	3	0.000	8	AL	3	0.000
9	OH	3	0.000	9	IL	3	0.000
10	TN	3	0.000	10	NY	3	0.000
11	KS	2	0.132	11	MT	2	0.087

Second Wave Policy Network				Third Wave Policy Network			
Rank	Court	Case Count	Prestige	Rank	Court	Case Count	Prestige
12	CT	2	0.113	12	MA	2	0.076
13	WY	2	0.094	13	KS	2	0.070
14	AR	2	0.057	14	WY	2	0.064
15	AK	2	0.000	15	AK	2	0.000
16	MA	2	0.000	16	AR	2	0.000
17	MT	2	0.000	17	CT	2	0.000
18	NE	2	0.000	18	NE	2	0.000
19	OR	2	0.000	19	OR	2	0.000
20	PA	2	0.000	20	PA	2	0.000
21	WI	1	0.132	21	KY	1	0.087
22	CA	1	0.113	22	NC	1	0.047
23	FL	1	0.000	23	VT	1	0.047
24	KY	1	0.000	24	SC	1	0.023
25	LA	1	0.000	25	CA	1	0.000
26	MD	1	0.000	26	FL	1	0.000
27	ME	1	0.000	27	LA	1	0.000
28	MI	1	0.000	28	MD	1	0.000
29	MN	1	0.000	29	ME	1	0.000
30	MO	1	0.000	30	MI	1	0.000
31	NC	1	0.000	31	MN	1	0.000
32	ND	1	0.000	32	MO	1	0.000
33	OK	1	0.000	33	ND	1	0.000
34	RI	1	0.000	34	OK	1	0.000
35	SC	1	0.000	35	RI	1	0.000
36	VA	1	0.000	36	VA	1	0.000
37	VT	1	0.000	37	WI	1	0.000
38	WA	0	0.113	38	CO	0	0.023
39	WV	0	0.094	39	DE	0	0.000
40	CO	0	0.000	40	GA	0	0.000
41	DE	0	0.000	41	HI	0	0.000
42	GA	0	0.000	42	IA	0	0.000
43	HI	0	0.000	43	IN	0	0.000
44	IA	0	0.000	44	MS	0	0.000
45	IN	0	0.000	45	NM	0	0.000
46	MS	0	0.000	46	NV	0	0.000
47	NM	0	0.000	47	SD	0	0.000
48	NV	0	0.000	48	UT	0	0.000
49	SD	0	0.000	49	WA	0	0.000
50	UT	0	0.000	50	WV	0	0.000

Turning now to our professionalism hypothesis, we note that New Jersey is ranked eighth overall in table 4.3. It is also important to note that many of the courts that are ahead of New Jersey have prestige scores of 0, suggesting that a professional court is unable to become prominent in the education policy network if cases are not brought before it. This leads us to reject our professionalism hypothesis, while also providing further support for our case volume hypothesis.

Table 4.3. Professionalism in the Citation Network

Rank	Court	Professionalism	Prestige Wave 2	Prestige Wave 3
1	CA	1.051	0.113	0.000
2	PA	1.007	0.000	0.000
3	MI	0.901	0.000	0.000
4	FL	0.828	0.000	0.000
5	SC	0.828	0.000	0.023
6	NY	0.818	0.000	0.000
7	WV	0.813	0.094	0.000
8	NJ	0.807	0.151	0.122
9	IL	0.803	0.000	0.000
10	LA	0.760	0.000	0.000
11	VA	0.731	0.000	0.000
12	WA	0.724	0.113	0.000
13	DE	0.711	0.000	0.000
14	OH	0.698	0.000	0.047
15	NH	0.694	0.000	0.070
16	TX	0.694	0.000	0.081
17	TN	0.676	0.000	0.070
18	CO	0.671	0.000	0.023
19	AZ	0.669	0.000	0.064
20	GA	0.660	0.000	0.000
21	NC	0.654	0.000	0.047
22	NM	0.650	0.000	0.000
23	MA	0.648	0.000	0.076
24	NE	0.641	0.000	0.000
25	IN	0.638	0.000	0.000
26	MD	0.631	0.000	0.000
27	WI	0.629	0.132	0.000
28	MN	0.627	0.000	0.000
29	CT	0.620	0.113	0.000
30	MO	0.598	0.000	0.000
31	KY	0.593	0.000	0.087
32	AR	0.583	0.057	0.000

Rank	Court	Professionalism	Prestige Wave 2	Prestige Wave 3
33	AK	0.580	0.000	0.000
34	KS	0.574	0.132	0.070
35	OR	0.546	0.000	0.000
36	RI	0.518	0.000	0.000
37	IA	0.458	0.000	0.000
38	AL	0.451	0.000	0.000
39	OK	0.441	0.000	0.000
40	MS	0.438	0.000	0.000
41	ID	0.436	0.000	0.023
42	ME	0.436	0.000	0.000
43	NV	0.407	0.000	0.000
44	MT	0.401	0.000	0.087
45	HI	0.394	0.000	0.000
46	WY	0.347	0.094	0.064
47	UT	0.320	0.000	0.000
48	SD	0.304	0.000	0.000
49	VT	0.297	0.000	0.047
50	ND	0.267	0.000	0.000

Finally, we examine our education provision hypothesis. Table 4.4 indicates that New Jersey has an education provision score of 2, which is the top score. This provides support for our expectation that those state supreme courts with the most extensive education finance provisions are the most likely to become prestigious in the education finance policy network.

Table 4.4. Professionalism in the Citation Network with Constitutional Provisions

Rank	Court	Education Provisions	Prestige Wave 2	Prestige Wave 3
1	NJ	2	0.151	0.122
2	WI	2	0.132	0.000
3	CA	2	0.113	0.000
4	CT	2	0.113	0.000
5	WA	2	0.113	0.000
6	WV	2	0.094	0.000
7	WY	2	0.094	0.064
8	AR	2	0.057	0.000
9	AL	2	0.000	0.000

continued on next page

Table 4.4. Continued.

Rank	Court	Education Provisions	Prestige Wave 2	Prestige Wave 3
10	AZ	2	0.000	0.064
11	DE	2	0.000	0.000
12	ID	2	0.000	0.023
13	IL	2	0.000	0.000
14	IN	2	0.000	0.000
15	KY	2	0.000	0.087
16	MD	2	0.000	0.000
17	MN	2	0.000	0.000
18	MT	2	0.000	0.087
19	NC	2	0.000	0.047
20	ND	2	0.000	0.000
21	NH	2	0.000	0.070
22	NM	2	0.000	0.000
23	OH	2	0.000	0.047
24	OR	2	0.000	0.000
25	PA	2	0.000	0.000
26	TX	2	0.000	0.081
27	VA	2	0.000	0.000
28	KS	1	0.132	0.070
29	AK	1	0.000	0.000
30	CO	1	0.000	0.023
31	FL	1	0.000	0.000
32	GA	1	0.000	0.000
33	LA	1	0.000	0.000
34	MA	1	0.000	0.076
35	ME	1	0.000	0.000
36	MI	1	0.000	0.000
37	MO	1	0.000	0.000
38	NE	1	0.000	0.000
39	NV	1	0.000	0.000
40	NY	1	0.000	0.000
41	OK	1	0.000	0.000
42	RI	1	0.000	0.000
43	SC	1	0.000	0.023
44	SD	1	0.000	0.000
45	TN	1	0.000	0.070
46	UT	1	0.000	0.000
47	VT	1	0.000	0.047
48	HI	0	0.000	0.000
49	IA	0	0.000	0.000
50	MS	0	0.000	0.000

Discussion and Conclusion

We have examined the predictors of prestige in the state supreme court education finance network from both a citation and policy perspective. With citations we find our proposed explanations generally fall short, at least with respect to descriptive statistics. By contrast, in the policy network our explanations, with the exception of professionalism, provide an accurate account of prestige in the network. Our findings provide support for an underlying critique in the literature of citation networks; a citation does not necessarily capture the influence that scholars attempt to explain.

Citations still hold value. Indeed, as noted by Choi et al. (2009), whether a citation is positive or negative, it still conveys influence over the content of an opinion. To this end, scholars have dedicated considerable attention to citations, but as our results and previous work by Gleason and Howard (2015) demonstrate, citations are complex and to truly understand how they work we must move beyond descriptive statistics. Yet, in contrast we note that the policy network renders very different results that support two of our three hypotheses even when relying on descriptive statistics. This seemingly suggests that policy is perhaps a more parsimonious explanation; or at the very least policy is a fundamentally different concept than citation. While policy is a more parsimonious explanation, it is hardly one that we can simply leave with this level of analysis. Accordingly, we now turn to a more in-depth exploration of the policy network in the next chapter.

Chapter 5

Policy Diffusion through Courts

Introduction: Do as I Do, Not as I Say

In this fourth empirical chapter we present an eagle-eyed view of court mandated education finance reform. Whereas we focused on state-bound environments to understand whether courts or legislatures are most likely to address education finance reform in chapter 2, and focused on citation behavior in chapter 3, here we take a closer look into the policy network we described in chapter 4. Whereas we presented a static description of the court network that mandated education finance reform in chapter 4, in this chapter we analyze why some courts choose to enter the policy network while others do not.

Ultimately, we are interested in tracing how court-ordered reform spreads across the United States. The citation network we presented in chapter 3 can be helpful in understanding how state courts communicate their choices. As we concluded, though, citation patterns explain the behavior of some courts in addressing education finance reform better than that of others. Accordingly, it presents a skewed view of how courts influence one another, leaving open the question of how court-mandated education finance policy spreads through the country. This chapter seeks to fill that void and centers on the fundamental question of court-mandated education finance reform: why do some courts follow the lead of other states, and why do others fail to do so?

To answer the preceding question, we investigate the *policy* network more closely—regardless of whether courts choose to cite preceding decisions. In other words, we look for connections between courts that have

Parts of this chapter are drawn from Howard, Roch, and Schorpp (2017).

mandated education finance reform rather than limit ourselves to courts that have cited sister courts' mandated education finance reform. We apply a theoretical framework first developed to explain legislative policy diffusion to state courts to understand which factors lead a court to adopt education finance reform before or after other courts have done so. Doing so allows us to understand how the policy itself diffuses across the American states. We first discuss what diffusion means and how it has been studied in the legislative context, followed by an application of diffusion theory on courts, and, finally, an analysis of the pattern of the policy diffusion we are studying in this book: court-mandated education finance reform.

Policy Diffusion in the States

Our federalist system allows policy differences, whether enacted by the legislature or ordered by the courts, between the states. What is more, several policy domains are left to the states, including such areas as marriage and divorce and, perhaps most prominently, education. Scholars have created an extensive literature examining these policy changes within states, but much of this literature focuses either on policy change through state legislatures or through state courts. Neither literature has incorporated findings from the other. As we showed in chapter 2, state court action in education finance reform occurred, in part, due to inaction by the legislature and the roadblock to the federal judiciary imposed by the *San Antonio Independent School District v. Rodriguez*[1] decision in 1973. With pressure to act and little guidance from the legislature, state courts have little but to look to one another.

State court literature, though, assumes that decisions reached by state courts of last resort are largely independent of other state courts of last resort. Each state court is assumed to confront different governors, publics, and state legislatures in rendering decisions and to have its own preferences, laws, and particular set of institutional constraints. Whether a court is asked to be the thirtieth or the first state to legalize marijuana for medical use, though, might enter the calculations of a judge in a moderate to conservative setting. The beginnings of state court-ordered education finance reform, following California's *Serrano v. Priest*[2] decision suggests such a calculation: "Because most other states' school finance systems resemble California's, the Serrano victory touched off a race for reform. Some fifty-two similar actions were promptly filed in thirty-one states. By 1977, at least twenty-five states (as many as thirty-one by some counts) had overhauled their financial structures to provide greater equity in education funding" (Carroll and Park 1983, 2). While state courts are arguably the political actors that are most isolated from external influences and most bound by state laws, most of the questions and problems they address are not unique to their state.

All this suggests that policy diffusion is a relevant framework in explaining state court decision-making in education finance reform. State policy decisions, diffusion scholars argue, are not independent of one another. Rather than assume that states are blind to how their neighbors tackle the problems they confront, they test to what degree state actors take into account the actions of other states. For example, Walker in his classic work noted that California's fair trade law was adopted in twenty other states and that states followed each other in the adoption of state highway departments (Walker 1969). Other scholars have noticed the diffusion of, among other things, antismoking policies (Shipan and Volden 2006).

One of the few efforts to model diffusion failed to show an influence on state court decisions by *neighboring* court decisions or *neighboring* legislative policy (Roch and Howard 2008; see also Canon and Baum 1981). Recent scholarship on policy diffusion, however, has reached beyond the simple concept of geography to focus on how states and nations learn from or emulate other states or nations as they look for leadership within a particular policy domain (Boehmke 2009; Shipan and Volden 2008; Walker 1969). As states face new or complex policy issues, they may seek guidance from fellow state governments. Instead of expecting diffusion to occur geographically, more recent research suggests that diffusion occurs among states that share similar characteristics or when a state has adopted a successful policy (Boehmke 2009; Volden 2006). Rather than spilling over borders, policies spread when policy innovations are actively sought out and emulated by other states.

We argue that policy diffusion occurs between state courts as well as state legislatures. State courts follow the lead of other state courts and adopt policy decisions of sister courts even though one state court is not bound by the holding or reasoning of a sister state court. They do so because the behavior of other state courts provides an informational short cut that judges can use when making policy decisions.

We argue that diffusion through state courts is an important part of explaining the history of education finance reform. As we noted, education finance reform has been largely left to the states in the aftermath of *San Antonio Independent School District v. Rodriguez* (1973), and empirical research shows that state courts have had a significant influence on the outcome of education finance reform (Wood and Theobald 2003; Murray, Evans, and Schwab 1998; Manwaring and Sheffrin 1997). Furthermore, education finance reform has occupied all states in some form. Judges have the potential to use information and data points of other states' efforts in reforming education finance as they contemplate decisions on the difficult topic. We start our analysis with that very point—by offering our theory on how and why state courts emulate sister state courts.

Diffusion and Emulation of Court-Ordered Education Finance Reform

At the end of the Warren court, Justice Brennan (1986) and others urged litigants to use state courts and state constitutions to protect rights and liberties (Solimine 2002; Pulliam 1999; Tarr 1998). The movement to equalize state education financing is consistent with and contemporaneous to this move to the New Judicial Federalism. With the *San Antonio Independent School District v. Rodriguez* (1973) decision foreclosing federal court relief, litigants began using state constitutions and asking state courts for relief. As a result, state courts would observe and discuss new ideas and make note of innovative approaches by other state courts as they determined their own rulings when confronted by state education finance reform litigation. For example in *Connecticut Coalition for Justice in Education Funding v. Rell* (2010),[3] the Connecticut court explicitly referenced its state constitution's educational provision and the similarly worded education provisions of other state constitutions.

This consideration of the ideas and actions of other state courts may have resulted in the emulation of the actions of other state courts, or policy diffusion. As defined by Berry and Berry (2014, 308), diffusion involves "government adoptions of policies as emulations of previous adoptions by other governments." This behavior is in part grounded in the idea that states often act as policy laboratories, where states consider "adopting novel policies to address their needs, abandoning unsuccessful attempts, and learning from the successes of similar states" (Volden 2006, 294). Previous research suggests that diffusion may occur because policy-makers learn about the success of the policy or because states simply choose to imitate the actions of other states that share similar characteristics without considering the effectiveness of the policy (Berry and Berry 2014, 310–311; Shipan and Volden 2008).

The decriminalization—and later legalization—of marijuana is an example of a policy that started in one or two states (policy laboratories) and that has since been emulated by other states, leading to the policy diffusion of marijuana laws.[4]

Scholars examining policy diffusion among legislatures have found patterns of emulation on a range of social and economic policies within the United States (Boehmke 2009; Shipan and Volden 2008; Volden 2006; Boehmke and Witmer 2004) as well as between nations (see, e.g., Gilardi, Füglister, and Luyet 2009; Elkins, Guzman, and Simmons 2006). The findings from this research suggest that state and federal governments are more likely to follow successful programs as well as other states and nations that have similar characteristics, such as a similar level of wealth or a shared ideology.

We argue that courts may use similar informational cues when considering education finance reform and that the behavior of sister state courts provides an informational short cut that courts can use when making policy decisions. Gibson (1983, 9) explains the influences on judges' decision-making as "a function of what they prefer to do, tempered by what they think they ought to do, but constrained by what they perceive is feasible to do." We expect policy diffusion to occur where the actions of sender state courts (the courts that first initiate reforms) can provide information on any of these three areas.

As Grossback et al. (2004, 523) argue, policy-makers "do not know the exact ideological position of the innovation. In an attempt to determine where the policy lies on the issue space, policy makers look to the ideological patterns of those who have previously adopted the policy." In other words, looking at what other courts have done helps judges to map their choice onto an ideological continuum and to make a more informed decision about which position is closer to their ideal point. As the consequences of these policies become better known, though, the marginal improvement this particular short cut provides will diminish.

Apart from providing cues on the ideological position of reform, the actions of sister courts can help assess how decisions fit into the legal and political constraints faced by the court. Besides their own preferences and the potential impact of the policy, judges have to consider how the public and the other branches of government will perceive their decision. Lacking majoritarian authority, a court ruling is riskier than actions undertaken by elected legislative bodies that have the democratic support of the larger electorate. Every court ruling can potentially weaken or strengthen a court's legitimacy, depending on how the ruling is perceived by the public and other political actors. Observing where sister state courts position themselves provides useful information, which is particularly helpful when new, unsettled, or vague policies are under consideration.

Strong legal authority for court action can influence the parameters in which the court operates as it considers its own preferences and potential political constraints. Courts that are acting on strong legislative or even constitutional provisions are less likely to operate within a vague policy environment. A court's action in conformity with legislative or constitutional provisions is also more likely to be perceived as legitimate. While these courts are therefore least dependent on cues from sister states, the context in which they successfully set policy becomes relevant information to their sister courts.

More generally, then, the decisions sender courts make and the contexts within which they make them provide multidimensional information to other courts about the policy itself and about the actors who support it. This information can be used when courts evaluate their options. Emulation can therefore be a function of informational scarcity when courts face unsettled policy as well as a tool of efficiency, providing easily accessible cues about the political viability of a given policy. It reduces uncertainty and therefore the risk of engaging in actions that will be challenged by the public or by other branches of government. Under this mechanism, a receiver state would choose to emulate a court that is ideologically proximate, faces similar constraints from the public and the elected branches, or is situated in a state with a similar economic position.

This emulation is closer to the "imitation" mechanism that Shipan and Volden (2008) offer as one of two mechanisms through which policy diffusion occurs. Contrary to the second mechanism, "learning," imitation occurs without knowledge of the effects of the policy. Learning, on the other hand, implies that the long-term effect is known and taken into consideration. While it is very well possible that policy diffusion through state courts may, under some conditions, also be a result of learning in the sense that Shipan and Volden (2008) use the word, the institutional features of courts make emulation or imitation more likely, as does the complex issue of education finance reform, which requires years or decades to evaluate. As Carroll and Park wrote more than a decade after these reform movements started:

> It is difficult to foresee the outcomes of any reform plan. Value judgments and political realities aside, people often disagree about the likely effects of various reform proposals, nor is the track

> record thus far very illuminating. The reforms that states have undertaken differ in degree and kind, but no consistent body of information has been compiled either on how well reforms have worked in the individual states or on the relative effects of various approaches to reform. (1983, 4)

By the time the policy consequences of a state court decision are sufficiently known to allow learning, other state courts are likely to have developed their own set of laws and precedents that limit state court choices and make learning both less profitable and less feasible. Courts are bound by the body of law developed in their own state; unlike legislatures, who are free to set policy at any point they wish, courts are limited by existing policies. While they can strike down laws and provide guidelines as to which policies pass muster, they are not free to move policy indiscriminately. This limitation lessens the practicability of long-term learning for court policy diffusion. In other words, in the case of courts, the more developed policies in the issue area are, the less likely policy diffusion will occur. The less developed jurisprudence is, the more likely emulation is to be both helpful and possible.

Political, Institutional, and Legal Factors Influencing Emulation

To determine factors influencing emulation, we will follow other diffusion scholars in applying a dyad-based approach. In a dyadic analysis, the units of observation are pairs of states, which allows for the examination of dyad-level characteristics: do states follow states that are similar? Instead of focusing on state-level predictors (e.g., educational spending for a given state), we will look at state pair differences (such as differences in educational spending between sender and receiver state).

States appear multiple times in the dataset—each state is paired as a sender state with all possible other states but also appears as a receiver state paired with all possible combinations of sender states. This approach allows researchers to test whether diffusion is more likely to occur between similar states (dyad-level measures), while also looking at the state characteristics for likely sender and likely receiver states. We argue, as do other scholars using a dyad approach, that many of the same characteristics that can affect whether a state chooses to adopt a particular policy innovation may also influence how states assess the actions of other states.[5] Thus, when assessing policy emulation among state courts, we consider many of the same factors that scholars typically consider when looking at those factors internal to the states that influence judicial decision-making.

Thus, when a court asks, "What are the reasons to engage in education finance reform within my state?," it is likely to examine, in addition to the ideological position of the proposed reform, the structure of the state constitutions within states that have ordered court reform, the extent of the problem, institutional constraints, other political solutions, and the local political environment.

Our theory suggests that courts will take cues from similarly situated sister courts and we therefore focus on the similarity between pairs of states. Dyadic models provide the advantage of allowing us to test hypotheses that predict which state court *pairs* are most likely to engage in court-mandated reform. We note that the motivation for following the court-mandated reform of sister states may differ depending on which wave the court-mandated reform occurs in. Where we expect differences depending on the wave of reform, we derive a separate set of hypotheses for each wave and justify our reasoning. We organize our expectations of those factors affecting emulation into three categories: legal, political, and socioeconomic characteristics.

Legal factors. Strong state constitutional provisions should matter to state courts of last resort, and this should particularly be so following the denial of federal equal protection. In the second wave, in particular, this was the first instance in which courts premised reform on state legal authority rather than federal law, and thus legal authority at the state level should be particularly important. Whether state constitutional language (Roch and Howard 2008), jurisprudential regimes (Richards and Kritzer 2002), or precedent (Bailey and Maltzman 2008), judges, to some extent, follow the law. Recent scholarship has shown that law, even after controlling for attitudes, matters to decisional outcomes (Bartels 2009; Bailey and Maltzman 2008; Richards and Kritzer 2002). For state education financing, an important consideration is the language of state constitutions. The contents of state constitutions vary considerably, often incorporating different language to articulate the legal rights of their citizens or extending overt protections that the US Constitution does not.

For example, almost all state constitutions have provisions guaranteeing free public education. While many of these speak only of the obligation to provide free education, several states have much more detailed provisions describing the funding of, or providing for, uniform or efficient free public schools and speak of justice and equality in education.[6] These legal provisions should act as a lens through which litigants and judges assess the degree of inequality within a state and decide whether inequalities are great enough to justify reform through the courts.

Clear legal authority should also provide legitimacy. Thus, when a state court uses its strong state constitutional provisions on education to order reform, other courts will likely perceive those actions as legitimate and as a basis for reform within their state, particularly if they possess similar provisions.

State courts have acknowledged the importance of the language of state educational constitutional provisions in other states. For example, in our previously discussed *Connecticut Coalition for Justice in Education Funding v. Rell* (2010), the Connecticut court explicitly referenced their state constitution's educational provision and the similarly worded education provisions of other state constitutions. The majority opinion noted, "We have discussed in detail . . . cases from states whose education clauses are worded and structured closely to article eighth, §1, of the constitution of Connecticut. The vast majority of the other states have reached the same conclusion, namely, that students are entitled to a sound basic, or minimally adequate, education in the public schools."

In sum, we expect that courts will be most likely to emulate courts that have mandated education finance reform with similar constitutional provisions. We expect that this is particularly likely to occur during the second wave of reform, with initial attempts to use state equal protection clauses giving way to the use of state education clauses.

Similar to constitutional provisions requiring adequacy, legislative reform provides a legal basis for the court to act. As we saw in chapter 2, whether due to strategic reasons, deference to the legislature, or because the problem is solved, if legislatively enacted school finance reform occurs, courts are less likely to order court reform during the second wave. For those that get involved regardless of legislative action, information provided by sister courts that have acted under similar circumstances will be particularly useful. Conversely, courts that operate without legislative guidance should be most likely to emulate courts that mandated education finance in the absence of legislative directive.

However, in the third wave, where courts are confronting the problem of enforcing their own decisions, we should see less emulation of legal authority. At this stage, the court of last resort now has its own precedent and authority to rely on for an adequacy decision. We therefore expect legal authority in the form of legislative statutes or constitutional provisions on education finance to present valuable information to courts in the second wave of reform, but less so in the third wave of reform.

Political factors. Our theory posits that actions by sister courts provide informational cues that can help receiver courts assess how decisions fit into the particular legal and political constraints they face. Ideological cues can help courts assess the probability of implementation of their decision. Scholars have shown that government preferences can constrain state courts (Johnson 2015; Langer 2002; Brace, Hall, and Langer 1998), which rely on the executive and the legislature to implement their decisions. Successful implementation of policy change is also dependent on public opinion (Taylor et al. 2012; Seeljan and Weller 2011; Stoutenborough and Beverlin 2008), which can constrain government action and promote enforcement of court decisions. To see whether education reform is feasible in their state, courts will look to the political constraints present in other states to better determine whether a given decision is politically viable in their state.

All other things equal, we expect courts that face higher political constraints (i.e., states in which judges are more ideologically distant to the population and the elected branches) to be more likely to profit from the information that the policy network provides than those who come from more ideologically homogeneous states. They gain most by waiting for courts with a range of political constraints to mandate education finance policy, providing them with examples of courts in different political contexts to evaluate and also point to, should they face criticism.

Elected judges are likely to pay particular attention to decisions other elected judges, who are similarly at risk of electoral retaliation, have handed down. For instance, research has shown retaliation by the public in the form of recall voting when judicial votes were inconsistent with public attitudes on the death penalty (Culver and Wold 1986). Elected judges do appear to alter their behavior in response to a perceived risk of electoral reprisal (Huber and Gordon 2004; Hall 2001). In their study of policy convergence between state supreme courts and the US Supreme Court, Kilwein and Brisbin (1997) also found some support for the role of the selection methods of state judges in doctrinal convergence and divergence. We think that this will hold true for both waves. We therefore expect that dyads are more likely to form between a receiver state court and a sender state court when both states have an appointed judiciary or when both states have an elected judiciary.

Receiver courts also perceive reform as less risky when they operate within a similar context. These stable environments are more likely to exist in the case of appointed rather than elected courts.

In chapter 3, we noted that court prestige helps explain patterns of citation in education finance reform. If prestige matters to the receiver state, it is likely to do so most when the sender is more prestigious than the receiver. Rather than expect emulation between state pairs with similar levels of prestige, we expect prestige to work in the opposite direction: emulation should be more likely between states with more disparate levels of prestige.

Socioeconomic factors. Courts may also choose to follow courts from states with similar economic characteristics, as seen in some of the state policy literature considering diffusion. These similarities should assure the receiver state court that they are following a court that may have similar resources for dealing with the problem at hand and may further assure the receiver state that the policy is defensible within their state. Research has shown that courts do take state wealth into account when making judicial decisions (Beavers and Walz 1998). Thus, state supreme courts should follow and be persuaded by courts that have adopted education finance reform and that reside in states with similar economic environments.

For institutions that deal with law and textual language, the magnitude of the problem should matter. That is, the size and magnitude of the variation in inequality of education finance should be a factor in determining the actions of both sender and receiver states (see, e.g., Komesar 1994; Hanushek 1991). We expect that emulation is more likely to occur between a receiver state and a sender state when both states have a greater disparity in education financing.

Finally, from previous examinations of courts and diffusion (Roch and Howard 2008; Canon and Baum 1981), we expect the actions of neighboring states to pressure courts less than they do legislatures. Courts are dependent on litigation occurring in their states and are less able to choose to follow the actions of their neighbors. Even if this opportunity arises, they should be more closely attuned to the actions of states with particular characteristics that will help assure them of a legitimate basis for the decisions that they make within their own states, such as states with similar educational clauses within their state constitutions, rather than following public opinion originating in a neighboring state in favor of court-mandated reform. Indeed, in their network analysis of persistent policy pathways in the American states, Desmarais, Harden, and Boehmke (2015) found that "the overwhelming majority of policy diffusion relations exist between states that are not geographically contiguous" (397). We therefore do not expect emulation to be more likely between neighboring states.

Data, Method, and Model

Our method is a dyad-year event history analysis.[7] To empirically examine the likelihood of court reform, we gathered state-level data from 1974 through 2010.[8] We start with 1974 because it is one year after the decision in *San Antonio Independent School District v. Rodriguez* (1973)—the start of the second wave of school finance reform and its emphasis on state constitutional provisions. We omit any analysis of the first wave because in the first wave there was no successful implementation of a federal equal protection right and, therefore, no successful emulation to model. Our two models then follow the time periods of each wave, with the second wave (Model 1) running until 1988 and the third wave running from 1989 until the end of our data. Each dependent variable is a dichotomous variable as to whether state education finance reform was adopted by the court and thus follows a probit model.

Our dataset consists of pairs of states (dyads), and each state is paired with all other states as a sender state and as a receiver state.[9] We only include dyads for sender states that have enacted education finance reform, thus providing other states a basis for emulation. For example, if New York enacts court-ordered reform, then we include New York in our dyads as a sender state and pair it with all other states, providing them the opportunity to copy New York in future years. If New York never enacted any court-ordered reforms, then we would not include any dyads in our analysis where New York was a sender state (but it would be included as a receiver state).[10] Boehmke (2009) suggests that failing to control for the opportunity to emulate may lead to imitation bias, in which, under certain conditions, dyadic event history models mistakenly show policy emulation.[11] We discuss how we limit the inclusion of cases a bit further after describing our set of dependent and independent variables. While this results in a loss of data, the remaining data still provide us with 4,231 and 14,290 observations for the second and third waves of education finance reform, respectively, and lessen the possibility of statistically significant but substantively meaningless results. The use of dyads allows us to investigate the effect of inter-dyad characteristics on the probability of emulation. For example, we can investigate the effect of contextual similarities between any two states—something that would not be possible using traditional models—using the dyadic approach. This approach also allows us to consider the role of individual state-level characteristics (such as the political environment for a given state) and to analyze whether these characteristics play a different role in sender and receiver states.

Dependent Variables

It is important to note that our dependent variable captures a diffusion or emulation process that we infer as occurring when we see receiver states copying leader states. This inference is similar to that which is made in more traditional diffusion models, where scholars typically model the likelihood of policy adoption as a function of the state's internal characteristics and external factors such as the policies held by neighboring states (see Berry and Berry 2014). Scholars in these cases similarly infer a diffusion process as occurring when states adopt the same policies as their neighbors.

The logic underlying our dependent variable closely follows that of Volden (2006) and Gilardi and Füglister (2008):

> Volden codes it 1 when the potential "receiver" makes its policy more similar to that of the "sender." . . . Since the focus is not on the bilateral relations among the two states but on the general diffusion process, the goal is then to detect systematic patterns in increased similarities, and to estimate the influence of various factors on the decisions of states to introduce policy changes that move them closer to other states. This permits one to make inferences about the underlying diffusion process, which, however, remains unobserved. (Gilardi and Füglister 2008, 419)

Thus, we created dependent variables to capture whether the receiving state supreme court with the subscript *r* emulates the sending, or leading, state supreme court with the subscript *s* and thus orders education finance reform. We read each court opinion on education finance reform and recorded whether the court mandated reform. We only pair receiver states with sender states that have previously enacted court-ordered reform in a given wave, providing sender states with the opportunity to emulate or follow this state.

These are dichotomous variables that take on a value of 1 when emulation occurs and the receiving court engages in education reform and a value of 0 otherwise. We created one variable for each wave of reform.

Legal Independent Variables

Difference in constitutional language. We coded state constitutions on the strength of their state education adequacy clauses (Roch and Howard 2008). For each state constitution, we coded the state as a 0 if the state constitution did not contain a clause providing for a right to a free public education, a 1 if the state constitution contained a clause providing for a right to a free public education, and a 2 if the section or clause contained specific language on funding or provided for a uniform or efficient funding.[12] We give some specific examples of this variation in language in note 4 in this chapter.

Difference in legislative reform. Whether or not legislative reform occurred in the state is captured as an indicator variable (1 if yes, 0 if no). We used previous research by Evans, Murray, and Schwab (1997) to provide a measure of the occurrence of legislative reform from 1974 to 1992. For the remaining years in our data, we relied on information provided by the National Center for Education Statistics that summarized the funding systems in each state in order to determine whether legislative reform occurred during the years 1993–2014.[13]

Difference in prestige. To incorporate our findings regarding citation patterns, we rely on each state court's measure of prestige as derived from the citation network in chapter 3. The measure indicates the degree to which a state court's decision to mandate education finance reform is cited by courts that followed suit. We use the absolute difference between the measured prestige for each sender-receiver dyad to investigate whether receiver courts are more likely to follow courts with similar or with disparate levels of prestige.

Political Independent Variables

Difference in selection mechanism. To detect whether courts are more likely to emulate courts that operate under the same incentive structure, we created a dummy variable that indicates whether judges in sender and receiver courts are selected via the same mechanism. If judges in sender and receiver states are subject to initial or retention elections (or if they are appointed in both), the variable is coded as 1, and 0 otherwise.

Political environment. We stated earlier that the information about the political environment in which courts that mandate education finance act can be particularly helpful to courts that face political constraints. Our hypothesis is therefore not based on a distance measure between the sender and receiver state, but rather suggests particular patterns among sender states on one hand and receiver states on the other. We accordingly include measures of court ideology and the political environment in which the court operates separately for sender and receiver states.

To capture the political environment, we use the combined average of the revised and updated citizen and governmental liberalism scores as developed and described by Berry and Berry (1998).[14] Both measures are bound by 0 and 100, with higher values representing more liberal citizens and governments, respectively. The resulting measure is therefore also bound by 0 and 100, where higher values represent a more liberal political environment.

Court liberalism. In addition, the benefit of using these state ideology scores is that they are strictly comparable to measures of state-level judicial ideology developed by Brace, Langer, and Hall (2000), which we use for the measures of judicial state ideology. These PAJID scores (party-adjusted judicial ideology) are determined by a method that uses the partisan affiliation of judges and the prevailing mass and elite ideology of the state. Similar to the Berry scores, the PAJID scores are bound by 0 and 100, with larger values representing more liberal courts.

*Political environment * court liberalism.* Our main interest, however, lies not in whether we see patterns among sender and receiver court ideology or their political environment, but whether we can identify how political constraints shape diffusion patterns. We interact our measures of political environment and court liberalism to be able to identify how, for example, liberal courts in a conservative environment (and vice versa) act.

Socioeconomic Independent Variables

Difference in the degree of disparity in education financing. We use the coefficient of variation in instructional expenditures as a measure of the extent of education financing inequality in a given state.[15] This coefficient calculates the ratio of the standard deviation of the distribution of education funds within a state to its mean and thus captures differences in school funding that are comparable across states.[16] The broader the distribution of education funds in a state—that is, the greater disparity there is between counties within a state—the larger the standard deviation becomes in relation to the mean. States with more pronounced inequality in education finance will have large coefficients of variation, whereas states with more equal distributions will have smaller coefficients of variation. For example, in 1992, Pennsylvania's and New York's scores were 0.05 and 0.28, respectively. This means that, on average, school districts spent 5 percent less or more than the state mean on education per pupil in Pennsylvania, but districts in New York deviated on average by 28 percent from the state mean, suggesting higher inequality.[17]

Difference in per capita income and state population. We used per capita income as a measure of state wealth and thus as a measure of the capacity to correct education resource inequality. In addition, we include state population as another measure of the capacity of states to correct education finance variation.

Neighboring states. We include the variable "neighbor" to indicate whether the states included within each dyad are geographical neighbors (1 if yes, 0 otherwise).

We also include in our model a count of the number of instances of court reform. Some states have reformed their education finance systems through court mandates multiple times during the periods that we examine, providing other states multiple opportunities to emulate their activities. For instance, the Texas Supreme Court first ruled in favor of reform in 1989 and then again in 1991 and 1992.[18] Thus, when looking at our second dependent variable, it is possible for receiver states in 1993 to emulate Texas's actions (when it is the sender state within the dyad) in 1989, 1991, or 1992 and for the dependent variable to equal 1. We distinguish among these types of policy adoptions by taking into account the number of previous instances of court-ordered reform within the state. It is also possible that the accumulation of court decisions on education finance reform in a single state increases the importance of that court's position within the diffusion network (see also Fowler et al.'s [2007] importance score of US Supreme Court citations). As with the other variables, we look at the absolute difference in the number of court-ordered reform between sender and receiver states, expecting diffusion to occur between states with greater difference.[19]

Model

As we mentioned previously, we only pair receiver states with sender states that have previously enacted court-ordered reform in a given wave. Unless a state enacts court-ordered reform, it cannot be considered a potential sender state. Once it does, it provides other states with the opportunity to emulate or follow it. Thus, states have the opportunity to follow sender states' behavior within the following year.

Finally, we add some additional methodological controls. The model examines the effect of these characteristics over time. To control for this we include spline variables for different sets of years (Beck, Katz, and Tucker 1998). We use these rather than time point dummies because of the existence of a number of years in which no court-ordered reform occurred as well as for the sake of efficiency, as we need fewer spline variables than time point dummy variables. Finally, we uniquely identify each dyad so that we are able to cluster our standard errors by dyad. Thus, the standard errors within our models are robust to correlations within these clusters. We provide a complete list of our variables in table 5.1.

Table 5.1. Summary Statistics (Mean with Standard Deviations in Parentheses)

	Second Wave	**Third Wave**
Emulating Dyads	0.021 (0.142)	0.038 (0.191)
Legislative Reform$_{(\lvert r\text{-}s \rvert)}$	0.017 (0.129)	0.022 (0.145)
Constitutional Provision$_{(\lvert r\text{-}s \rvert)}$	0.533 (0.553)	0.533 (0.549)
Count of Court Reform$_{(\lvert r\text{-}s \rvert)}$	1.081 (0.665)	1.887 (1.425)
Education Variation$_{(\lvert r\text{-}s \rvert)}$	0.079 (0.079)	0.085 (0.078)
Total Population$_{(\lvert r\text{-}s \rvert)}$	6.875 (8.858)	5.922 (6.254)
Per Capita Income$_{(\lvert r\text{-}s \rvert)}$	3.188 (2.362)	6.289 (5.234)
Elected Court$_{(\lvert r\text{-}s \rvert)}$	0.509 (0.500)	0.500 (0.500)
Court Ideology$_{(s)}$	0.438 (0.225)	0.406 (0.221)
Political Environment$_{(s)}$	0.530 (0.164)	0.494 (0.217)

continued on next page

Table 5.1. Continued.

	Second Wave	**Third Wave**
Court Ideology$_{(r)}$	0.413 (0.198)	0.407 (0.198)
Political Environment$_{(r)}$	0.489 (0.175)	0.499 (0.196)
Prestige$_{(\|r-s\|)}$	0.022 (0.016)	0.026 (0.021)
Neighbor	0.069 (0.253)	0.092 (0.289)

Results

We can think of the findings of our diffusion model as clues to the timing of court-ordered reform within the policy network. Some characteristics may be important to understand the general likelihood of court-ordered education finance reform, and we discussed those implications in chapter 2. We found, for example, that states in which the legislature implemented education finance reform are less likely to also see court involvement in reform.

Here, we use some of the same characteristics to understand patterns in the network. If legislative reform fails to reach significance in the emulation models, that does not mean that legislative action is not important in predicting court behavior; it does, however, suggest that legislative action has no influence in the timing of reform. Courts in states that have passed legislative education finance reform are neither more likely to be leader states nor more likely to be followers. The presence of states with legislative reform on either (or both) sides of the dyad would, under those circumstances, be consistent with a random spread through the dataset—both as leader and as follower—and within the dyads—where legislative reform in the leader state is not more likely to be paired with legislative reform in the follower state. The model, then, states more about whether certain features are more likely among sender or receiver states (particularly in the case of variables that are not measured on the dyadic level, such as the political variables), as well as which shared (or opposed) characteristics within the dyads predict emulation (in the case of our dyad-level variables). With these caveats in mind, we proceed to discuss the findings for our models for the two waves of education finance reform.

What do leader and sender states dyads look like? We hypothesized that courts were most likely to emulate sister courts with similar contextual characteristics. Our findings suggest a more complex story. Table 5.2 represents the results of our regression predicting emulation between state pairs for the second wave (Model 1) and the third wave (Model 2). For the variables that represent absolute distances in the measure between sender and receiver states, negative findings suggest emulation to be more likely between more similar states and positive findings suggest emulation to be more likely between more disparate states. We discuss findings for the second wave and third wave in turn.

The first coefficient estimate in table 5.2 shows that diffusion in the second wave happens as state courts emulate sister courts that operate under

Table 5.2. Regression Results for Emulation (Pro Petitioner Only)

DV: Emulation	**Second Wave**	**Third Wave**
Legislative Reform$_{(\lvert r\text{-}s\rvert)}$	–3.740***	–0.027
	(0.098)	(0.139)
Constitutional Provision$_{(\lvert r\text{-}s\rvert)}$	–0.131	–0.042
	(0.092)	(0.048)
Count of Court Reform$_{(\lvert r\text{-}s\rvert)}$	–0.503***	–0.100***
	(0.078)	(0.020)
Education Variation$_{(\lvert r\text{-}s\rvert)}$	–1.323	–0.318
	(0.807)	(0.304)
Per Capita Income$_{(\lvert r\text{-}s\rvert)}$	0.037	0.029***
	(0.023)	(0.005)
Total Population$_{(\lvert r\text{-}s\rvert)}$	0.004	0.014***
	(0.006)	(0.003)
Elected Court$_{(\lvert r\text{-}s\rvert)}$	0.048	–0.065
	(0.108)	(0.053)
Court Ideology$_{(s)}$	0.326	0.337
	(0.857)	(0.274)
Political Environment$_{(s)}$	0.556	–0.287
	(0.789)	(0.245)
Court Ideology$_{(s)}$* Political Environment$_{(s)}$	–0.868	–0.240
	(1.507)	(0.474)

continued on next page

Table 5.2. Continued.

DV: Emulation	Second Wave	Third Wave
Court Ideology$_{(r)}$	4.205***	1.604***
	(0.958)	(0.273)
Political Environment$_{(r)}$	1.943**	0.390+
	(0.689)	(0.203)
Court Ideology$_{(r)}$* Political Environment$_{(r)}$	–5.041***	–1.716***
	(1.458)	(0.418)
Prestige$_{(\|r\text{-}s\|)}$	2.460	–2.836*
	(3.264)	(1.392)
Neighbor	–0.300	0.069
	(0.228)	(0.093)
Constant	–59.053	444.874***
	(218.623)	(86.874)
Observations	4231	14290
Log Pseudolikelihood	–362.09	–2168.95
AIC	762.18	4375.90
BIC	882.83	4519.67

Probit regression models with clustered standard errors (around dyad) in parentheses.
*$p < 0.05$, **$p < 0.01$, ***$p < 0.001$ (two-tailed).

the same statutory foundation. As we showed in chapter 2, court-mandated reform is more likely where statutory reform failed. Our findings suggest that this is true for both sender and receiver states. Emulation dyads are most likely where legislatures in neither sender nor receiver states have acted.[20] This makes intuitive sense: courts without legislative guidance may find the most to gain in imitation as they look to states that have acted under similar pressure in the past.

We also expected emulation to be more likely between state court pairs working under a similar constitutional mandate regarding education finance. Our results do not offer sufficient support for that hypothesis. While court-mandated reform, as we saw in chapter 2, is more likely to occur in states that provide a constitutional provision mandating equal educational access, our findings here suggest that there is no discernible pattern in how each dyad forms with regard to the constitutional framework of its two parts. Receiver states without such constitutional provisions are equally likely to follow sender states with as they are to follow those without the same provisions (and vice versa).

We find that courts follow courts with similar numbers of prior decisions regarding education finance reform, potentially suggesting a two-tracked diffusion pattern: one between state courts that are highly involved in reforming education finance and repeatedly rule in favor of reform, and another for courts that are represented in the dataset with one (or at most two) decisions within the second wave.

We fail to find evidence for our hypotheses that receiver state courts are more likely to follow courts with similar total populations, per capita income, or comparable disparity in education finance, suggesting that characteristics that might point to similarities in the problem that the court is asked to address are not helpful guides to receiver states.

The political environment matters. In chapter 2, we showed that liberal courts, all other things equal, were more likely to mandate reform than conservative courts. Our dyadic model instead looks to patterns among sender states and among receiver states.

While we find that sender courts do not share common policy preferences or political constraints, receiver courts do. In other words: there is a pattern to which state courts emulate courts that have mandated education finance reform and are therefore more likely to wait and follow than to lead or not to mandate reform at all. These significant coefficient estimates therefore suggest a strategic component in the calculations of courts.

To better understand the substantive effect of our political variables, we graphed their effect by looking at values of interest for court liberalism and the political environment (figures 5.1 and 5.2).

Figure 5.1 plots the probability of emulation for any given dyad (y-axis) across all values for our measure of political environment from most conservative (lowest value) to most liberal (highest value). The solid line plots probabilities for conservative receiver courts and the dashed line for liberal courts (where gray shaded area and dotted lines represent 95 percent confidence intervals, respectively). To calculate the predicted probabilities, we set all other variables to their respective mean values and define a liberal and a conservative court to be the seventy-fifth and twenty-fifth percentile of the court liberalism measure (0.25 and 0.55, respectively).

As may be expected, all other things equal, a conservative court is less likely to be a receiver state and emulate a sister court that has mandated education finance reform. As the political environment in which the

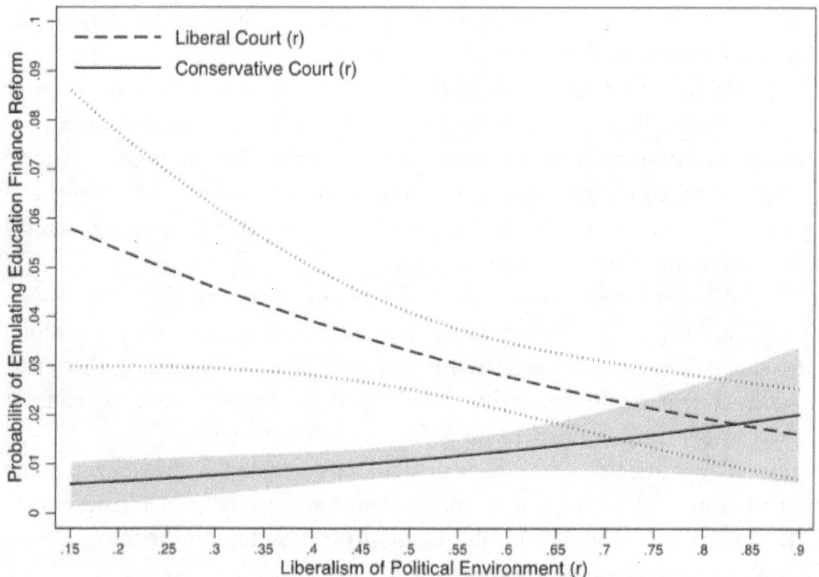

Figure 5.1. The Impact of Liberalism in the Political Environment of the Receiver State on the Probability of Emulation by Court Liberalism (Wave 2).

conservative court (solid line) is situated becomes more liberal, though, the probability of emulation raises slightly.

A liberal court, on the other hand, is more likely to emulate a sister court's decision when the political environment is conservative than when it is liberal. While liberal courts are more likely to mandate reform (see chapter 2), those facing a conservative public and government are most likely to be followers. This makes intuitive sense, as we would not expect courts with these constraints to be sender states but rather to wait until court-mandated education finance reform has been implemented in other parts of the country. The findings therefore suggest that, rather than being randomly distributed in the dyadic dataset, these particular political constellations are most likely to be found in receiver states.

A different way to interpret the interactive finding is to plot the influence of court liberalism on emulation for a conservative (solid line) and a liberal (dashed line) state separately (see figure 5.2). We can again see that, regardless of how liberal the citizens and the government are, more liberal courts are generally more likely to emulate sister courts that have mandated reform (since both lines rise as court liberalism increases). However, while the rise is small and steady for courts in liberal states, it is steeper for

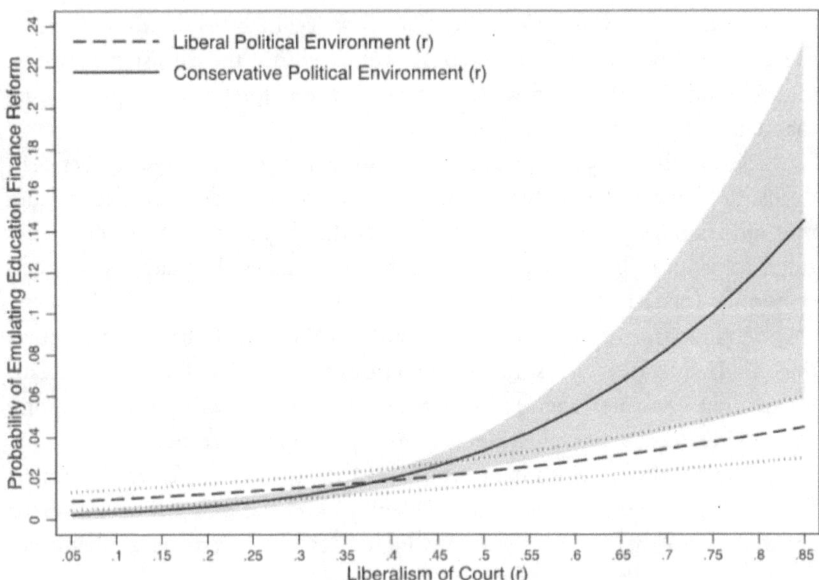

Figure 5.2. The Impact of Court Liberalism of the Receiver State on the Probability of Emulation by Political Environment (Wave 2).

those in a conservative environment. Similarly, while conservative courts (left side of the graph) are more likely to be followers when they are in a liberal environment, liberal courts (right side of the graph) are more likely to be followers in a conservative political environment. All of this suggests that followers are most likely to be found among those that are politically constrained. Rather than moving first, or randomly throughout the second wave of reform, these courts seem to wait until others have mandated reform to then emulate those courts.

We furthermore find that neighboring states are no more likely to form pairs than non-neighboring states, and that no predictable pattern exists with respect to a state court's perceived prestige. While citation patterns among courts that order education finance reform are dependent on prestige (see chapter 3), the diffusion of education finance policy seems to occur independently of the prestige of participating state courts.

Our findings for the third wave depart somewhat from our second wave findings (see Model 2 in table 5.2). None of the variables capturing legal factors predict the probability of emulation. By this point, leaders and followers who have and have not seen statutory reform and who rely on constitutions that do or do not contain education clauses seem randomly distributed across dyads, suggesting that these legal factors do not determine the timing or position of a state court's ruling within the diffusion network. Considering that the third wave centers on the enforcement of prior court mandates, this finding is not surprising.

Similar to the second wave, emulation is more likely to occur between dyads that have implemented a similar number of court decisions, suggesting that diffusion seems to occur among states that have either both repeatedly ruled for education finance reform or between states that have both ruled only once (or twice).

Against our expectations, courts are not most likely to emulate courts that reside in states with similar populations with similar incomes. Instead, we see that opposites seem to attract: dyads are most likely to form among states with disparate population sizes and per capita incomes.

The political environment influences the diffusion of reform in similar fashion as in the second wave: court ideology and the political environment matter, as does their interactive effect. Figure 5.3 plots predicted probabilities for the political variables of the receiver state.

As figure 5.1 did for the second wave, figure 5.3 plots the predicted probability for emulation in the third wave across values of state liberalism

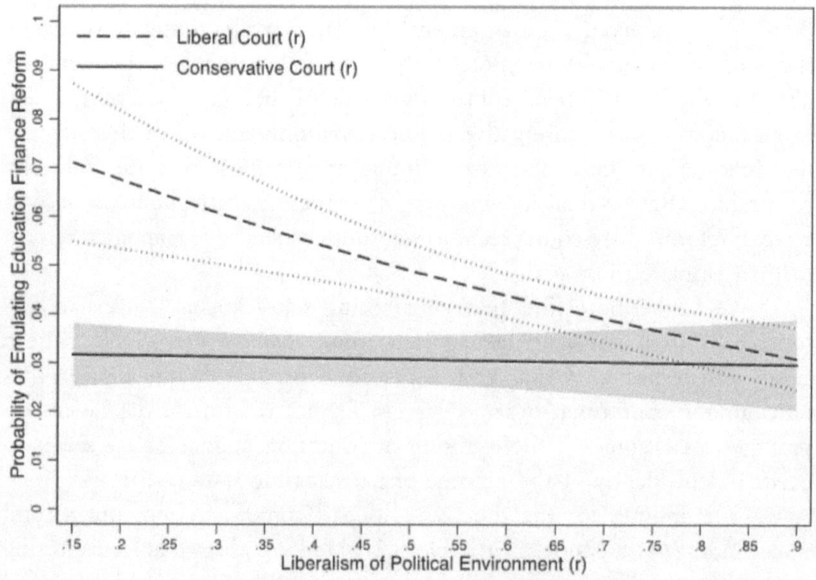

Figure 5.3. The Impact of Liberalism in the Political Environment of the Receiver State on the Probability of Emulation by Court Liberalism (Wave 3).

(citizens and government) for liberal (dashed line) and conservative (solid line) courts. Whereas the probability of emulation is constant for conservative courts regardless of how liberal the state it resides in is, liberal courts are generally more likely to emulate education finance reform and are more likely to be followers the more conservative the state is (left side of the graph).

For the third wave, we again find no higher likelihood of emulation between neighboring states, but prestige seems to matter in the third wave. Emulation dyads are more likely to form among state courts with similar levels of prestige, which suggests that different motivations inform the decision to emulate the policy and to cite the court once the court chooses to mandate education finance reform. The fact that legal factors do not matter in predicting emulation dyads in the third wave but political factors do is in line with this finding.

Following a court with high prestige seems to matter only to those who are also considered prestigious, suggesting that both citation and emulation are in part informed by the reputation of the court. We suggested in chapter 3 that citations are a tool of legitimization. Courts cite to signal that their decisions are in line with legal standards elsewhere and thus preempt potential criticism—which is particularly useful when the cited court is highly respected.

Our findings suggest that this is a tool courts use in emulation, too, though its use is limited to courts who have a reputation to uphold among their peers. In theory, prestigious courts should be least likely to benefit from following other prestigious courts, if their motivation for doing so is to legitimize their decision. However, if emulation is, as we explain, a result of courts seeking informational shortcuts, the observed pattern makes sense: prestigious courts will follow other prestigious courts, knowing that their position in the network is not jeopardized, since other prestigious courts have mandated education finance reform, too. In other words, as courts contemplate education finance reform and look to see what others like them have done, they include the level of prestige in their calculation of what a similar court is. The prestige network, then, is important both in the citation network and in explaining emulation between courts (in the third wave), though it serves a different purpose in each.

Discussion

State courts are, similar to state legislatures and governors, institutions created in service of state policy. That policy, though, is often not state specific in the broad sense. Most of the questions that state courts address involve policies that are debated or settled throughout the nation, suggesting either that courts must ignore the potential sources of information that other state institutions can provide or that courts are aware of policy debates and decisions in other states and that this awareness may, in turn, affect their own behavior.

We have argued that the latter is more likely and started the chapter introducing policy diffusion as a potential mechanism that explains court behavior within the national network of state court decisions. Our goal was twofold: to understand how courts use the state information that is available to them and to understand which factors are related to the diffusion of education finance policy across the nation. More specifically, we wanted to know where courts decide to position themselves within the network of education finance policy and how that in turn influences the diffusion of that policy.

Our findings suggest that courts are aware of the behavior of their peers, which, in turn, provides cues to the court about their own *and* other state courts' positions—with their idiosyncratic legal, political, and ideological predispositions—within the larger education finance policy network.

When policy and legal guidance from within the state are lacking (which is particularly true in the second wave), courts can and do look beyond their own borders as they contemplate the position of the policy. This is particularly true for courts who face political constraints and who strategically position themselves as receiver states, when education finance reform has been mandated by courts with a range of political constraints. At this point, the receiver courts have information that a number of courts have acted (and know the immediate reaction), and that information can potentially be useful to their allies as points of comparison, should they face backlash.

Chapter 6

Conclusion—How State Courts Move and Change Policy

Law, Politics, and Policy Formation

If one observed recent US Supreme Court nomination and confirmation battles, one could easily conclude that the judiciary is completely partisan and ideological. That is, a judge or justice is just a politician who has policy preferences, wants to implement those preferences, and can do so without electoral consequences or going through the trials and tribulations of the legislative process.

Federal judges have life tenure and independence. Article 3, section 1 of the United States Constitution states, "The Judges, both of the supreme and inferior Courts, shall hold their Offices during good Behaviour, and shall, at stated Times, receive for their Services, a Compensation, which shall not be diminished during their Continuance in Office." When the judges sit as Justices of the Supreme Court of the United States, they sit atop the judicial hierarchy with few realistic constraints. Constitutional decisions require almost impossible conditions to overturn,[1] and even statutory rulings require partisan and ideological alignment as well as policy agreement between Congress and the presidency. While there is debate on the influence of public opinion on the courts, there is no reason for life tenured judges to be overly concerned with public opinion.

It is a given that federal courts, and in particular the Supreme Court, make, influence, and create social and public policy. Abortion and gay marriage are just two areas where Supreme Court rulings have had an enormous impact. It is the general acceptance of the ideological nature of their rulings and the subsequent impact on policy that has led to such critical scholarly and public examinations of the Supreme Court nomination and confirmation process. A Merrick Garland as the median justice would have been very different than now having Chief Justice Roberts as the median justice.

State court judges, in contrast, confront a much different, and usually much more difficult, political environment. Either through having to face voters or mandatory retirement age, state court judges do not enjoy life tenure. The process of obtaining a seat on the highest court in each state greatly varies, with some appointed by merit and subject to retention elections, some confronting contested elections, others dealing with nonpartisan elections, still others subject to appointment, or reappointment. Many states allow state constitutional amendments through voter initiatives or other ballot measures, and in many states it is much easier to recall state court judges.

While we accept that judges on state courts of last resort have policy preferences, because state court judges confront much different pressures than federal court judges, state court judges have to be much more strategic in their dealing with the other institutions of government and much more receptive and concerned with public opinion if they wish to continue in office. As we have seen throughout the book, these courts often are indirectly or directly called upon to resolve policy issues because the state constitutions mandate that they do so, or because the other branches of state government fail to act and want the courts to resolve the issue. These courts cannot avoid issues and avoid having to confront an environment where the imposition of policy preferences becomes one of seeking the best outcome possible instead of the most preferred outcome.

This is particularly so in the policy issue that we examine—financing public education. As we have noted, public education depends in significant measure, almost one-half of funding, on local revenue sources, primarily taxes on homes and businesses. The greater the value of the properties, the more money is available for school funding.

Of course the problem is that property values are reliant, in large part, on quality schools. Higher-quality schools lead to higher property values. Wealthier and more politically aware individuals tend to live in more expensive homes in more expensive neighborhoods. Because of this you often have well-funded and very galvanized opposition to any change in school funding formulas. Political actors who seek to change the funding formula often do so at a significant cost to electoral positions.

The perils of changing funding formulas goes beyond just arousing the opposition of well-to-do homeowners. For most Americans who own their own home, a significant portion of their entire net worth is tied to home ownership. According to the census, the median net worth of all Americans is $68,828. However, this net worth includes a substantial portion from the equity Americans have in their individual home. The median net worth excluding equity is $16,942. Thus, this means that one's home is 75.39 percent of one's total net worth (Wang 2017). These numbers increase with age, meaning as one gets older, one's equity in one's home increases, and with most seniors retired, there is no additional earned income. Thus for people over the age of seventy, a home is over 80 percent of net worth.

So not only do quality schools increase the value of a home, quality schools also significantly increase total net worth. What this means is that any plan to reorganize or change the way schools are financed will confront significant opposition not just from organized interests such as teachers' unions and real estate professionals, but from homeowners anxious about how any change in financing might impact the value of their home and their overall net worth.

Of course, as we note in our introductory chapter, the United States is a nation that is deeply committed to the idea of education. We see it as a foundation for good citizenship and opportunity. Education is viewed as the great equalizer or leveler allowing all, even those who come from modest or poor backgrounds, to succeed in the marketplace of ideas, work, and wealth accumulation. So Americans pay homage to the idea of education, and we can see this in the state constitutional guarantees of a free public education.

However, while we support the idea of a quality free public education for students, of course, public education is not really free. Taxpayers must pay for public education. Since Americans support having local control of education, paying for public education means relying on local financing (i.e., property taxes) sources. However, as we have seen, relying on local sources can lead to significant inequality. These oftentimes competing ideas of local control and financing and quality free public education mean significant balancing of law, education policy, state court preferences, and the preferences of other states and state high courts.

From this we can understand why legislatures have been reluctant to take the lead on proposing education finance reform. If legislative reform is a rare occurrence (and we note the conditions needed for legislative reform in chapter 2), this means that those seeking to change school funding formulas must seek court reform. Once federal constitutional remedies were eliminated by the Supreme Court in 1973, this means initiating litigation and seeking relief from the state courts. Sometimes, as we have seen, this is an option favored by the other political actors. The legislature declines to move on changing the funding formula because of the various groups who favor the status quo, but it might support the courts ordering such a change. The caveat to that is the state-court-ordered policy change must fall within the policy space favored by the other institutional political actors if the justices wish to remain in office. If not, you can have situations such as Kansas or Nevada where the court decision is overridden, or the judges themselves are threatened with removal or loss of institutional power.

As long as government services (including public education) remain popular while the necessary measures to fund them remain deeply unpopular, courts will continue to play a role in determining the balance between defending constitutional (or statutory) mandates on one hand and directing the enforcement of unpopular funding mandates—with little visible power—on the other. Our book dives into the causes that place courts in such a position and into the factors that judges need to consider to come up with a realistic choice set of options, given their lack of purse and sword. Placed in the context of our analyses, the choices by Kansas and Nebraska judges, as we laid them out in chapter 1, can be explained by institutional, legal, and political factors. In both states, supreme court judges are appointed through a merit commission system. In both states, inequality in education funding within the state had grown in the years leading up to supreme court involvement. The combination of these factors made involvement by the court, as we lay out in chapter 2 (and as figure 2.4 shows) more likely. The addition of constitutional protections, furthermore, gives courts an added source of power in setting education finance policy.

Chapter 5 similarly predicts that liberal courts embedded in a conservative political environment (as in the case of Kansas), are most likely to follow sister courts in mandating education finance reform, suggesting that they are more likely to act after other courts have mandated education finance reform. This can provide courts in more hostile environments with some low-cost information and legitimacy in moving forward with court-mandated reform.

In each chapter we set out to demonstrate a specific instance of this interaction with other branches. We then examine the subsequent policy balancing by the courts, including relying on the authority of other state courts, and ultimately how they examine the policy environment of the other states and how those courts ultimately resolved this issue. We now review our findings for each empirical chapter.

Empirical Findings

Chapter 2: Why Courts?

In our first empirical chapter, we considered the strategic and interactive process of the court and another branch of government—the legislative branch—within the state environment and noted the differences between lawmaking and adjudication. We noted how legislatures and courts are different and react to different state factors. However, we also found that the more a court's institutional court structure resembles the structure of a legislature, that is, if the court is elected, the distinctions between them become less stark.

We found that the legislature defers to the court on education finance reform when the court is elected, and thus presumably shares the same policy preferences. However, that was not the complete story. Law and educational funding disparities matter greatly to appointed courts. An appointed court was more likely to intervene in education finance the greater the variation in educational expenditure throughout the state and the clearer the constitutional framework. Given these conditions, and the strategic deference of the legislature, it was not surprising that we saw much more court-ordered finance reform than legislative reform.

Chapter 3: Citation Patterns in Education Finance Policy

Our next question was, given a state court called upon to decide the thorny question of education finance reform, what does the state court look to or for in helping it decide whether to change the funding formula? That is, what sources of authority can a state court use, particularly if there is little or no precedent in the state itself? Thus we looked to citation patterns of these courts to determine if other state courts are very influential.

While our findings showed that some courts are more prestigious than others, suggesting their relative significance in influencing the legal reasoning within the network of education finance reform, our results failed to find one causal factor, and we note that these results suggest that citation prestige and authority might not be the causal factor in determining a state court's ruling on education finance reform.

We suggest several possible reasons for this. The first explanation is the one posited by Gleason and Howard (2015). Citations are driven by the interplay of a number of predictors for both the citing and cited court. For example, they note more extensive constitutional provisions increase the propensity of a court to cite a peer, but constitutional provisions have no bearing on whether a court is cited in the third wave. Thus, descriptive statistics cannot provide an adequate explanation for prestige and more methodologically rigorous explanations for what drives prestige are required. Yet, rather than go down that path, we think it is important to think about alternative conceptualizations of prestige that do not involve citations. Indeed, a host of literature suggests citations are not the ideal way to examine cross-court influence in the education finance network, and thus we demonstrate this in the next chapter, chapter 4.

Chapter 4: When Citations Are Not Enough

As noted, our analysis of citations finds that our proposed explanations generally fall short of showing influence. By contrast, in the policy network our explanations, with the exception of professionalism, provide an accurate account of prestige in the network. Our findings provide support for an underlying critique in the literature of citation networks: a citation does not necessarily capture the influence that scholars attempt to explain.

Citations still hold value. Indeed, as we note by citing Choi, Gulati, and Posner (2009), whether a citation is positive or negative, it still conveys influence over the content of an opinion. To this end, scholars have dedicated considerable attention to citations, but as our results and previous work by Gleason and Howard (2015) demonstrate, citations are complex and to truly understand how they work we must move beyond descriptive statistics. Yet, in contrast we note that the policy network renders very different results that support two of our three hypotheses even when relying on descriptive statistics. This seemingly suggests that it is perhaps a more parsimonious explanation, or at the very least this diffusion-based network is a fundamentally different concept than one based on citations. Even if it is a more parsimonious explanation, it is hardly one that we can simply leave with this level of analysis. Accordingly, we now turn to a more in-depth exploration of the policy network in the next chapter.

Chapter 5: Policy Diffusion through Courts

Since citations are not the causal factor in education finance decisions by state courts, to what then do state courts look to aid in their decisions? This chapter examines the influence of other states by examining the process of policy diffusion. Most analyses of state courts and decision-making tend to ignore the influence of other state courts except as examined in our chapter 3, which examines the influence of other state courts through citation analysis. This would wrongly suggest that state courts are ignoring the potential sources of information that other state institutions can provide.

Instead, we have argued that state courts are aware of policy debates and decisions in other states and that this awareness, in turn, influences their own decisions. Thus we start this chapter by introducing policy diffusion as a potential mechanism that explains court outcomes within the national network of state court decisions.

Our goal is both to understand how courts use the state information that is available to them and to understand which factors are related to the diffusion of education finance policy across the nation. While we acknowledge throughout that the book that courts are different and the law, and therefore precedent, matters, we also acknowledge that the courts as a policy-making institution will look to more than just the law. Specifically, we wanted to know where courts decide to position themselves within the network of education finance policy and how that in turn influences the diffusion of that policy.

We find that courts are aware of the behavior of their sister state courts, and this awareness provides informational cues to the court about its own and other state courts' positions considering their idiosyncratic legal, political, and ideological predispositions within the larger education finance policy network. Particularly when policy and legal guidance from within the state are lacking, courts can and do look beyond their own borders as they contemplate changing education finance policy. This is particularly true for courts who face political constraints and who strategically position themselves as receiver states, when education finance reform has been mandated by courts with a range of political constraints. At this point, the receiver courts have information that a number of courts have acted. This allows them to have an idea of what the reaction to the decision will be, and that information can be useful to supporters of the decision, should the court decision lead to a backlash.

What We Know

As we noted in our opening chapter, the debate over education funding provides insight into the creation and change of public policy. We chose public education finance reform as the focus of this examination because we wanted to understand both how and why courts can change public policy and how courts can change education policy as the courts interact with the other branches of government. In particular, education finance reform allows us to focus on state courts and allows us to compare responses across all the states in the union.

Education finance reform touches most aspects of American political life and when courts get involved, even elected ones, these courts confront pressures and deal with considerations that separate the courts from the other institutions of the American political system. Courts, of course, are political actors and electoral courts are greater political actors than appointed courts. While this is common knowledge to political scientists, much of the public, and many in the legal profession, cling to the idea that courts are neutral arbiters of the law, despite the hue and cry over US Supreme Court nominations.

However, while courts make political decisions, this is far from a complete picture of how courts change and influence policy. Courts are legal actors and do care about law. Text and precedent do seem to matter, at least in the form of textual commitments from state constitutional language, and of course any opinion cites precedent, both from prior decisions of the state court and decisions from sister state courts. These courts are often forced to make these decisions because the legislatures have been unwilling to act and litigants, relying on state educational clauses, have brought suit in state courts.

We have learned, however, that the citation of precedent from sister state courts has limited value as a causal factor in the state court decision. This is not to say that the decisions of other state courts do not matter. On the contrary, what other courts do is crucial to a state court that is confronted with needing to decide. These *receiver* state courts, which are those state courts needing to make decision, look at political, economic, and social characteristics of *sender* state courts, that is to say, those courts that have ruled on education financing. We show that these courts are influenced by those factors and the success of these sender courts in changing education finance policy.

We also examined the idea of "waves" of education finance reform and, in particular, we focused on the second and third waves. To review, the first wave began in the late 1960s and was premised on the equal protection clause of the Fourteenth Amendment to the United States Constitution. When this remedy was eliminated because of the *San Antonio Independent School District v. Rodriguez* decision, the second wave began. The next wave of cases rested primarily on state education clauses and state equal protection clauses and lasted until 1989. The third wave focused on specific adequacy provisions of state constitutions and continues to the present day. In these latter decisions we see continual litigation as plaintiffs use the state courts to prod the legislature to remedy what the plaintiffs see as failing to provide an adequate education. It is also this latter wave that has resulted in the clashes between the state courts and the other branches of state government.

Not all scholars agree with the concept of dividing litigation into waves. However, our empirical results do suggest that the ordering of these cases into waves has merit. We note, for example, in our analysis of citation patterns that what makes a court prestigious in the second wave may altogether differ from what makes a court prestigious in the third wave. We also find that the third wave network is considerably denser than the second wave network.

In our final empirical chapter, the emulation chapter, we noted some similarities and some differences between the waves. Specifically, in contrast to the second wave, in the third none of our hypothesized legal factors predict the probability of emulation. We argued that this is because by the third wave, leaders and followers who have and have not seen statutory reform and who rely on constitutions that do or do not contain education clauses, seem randomly distributed across dyads, suggesting that these legal factors do not determine the timing or position of a state court's ruling within the diffusion network. Considering that the third wave centers on the enforcement of prior court mandates, this finding is not surprising.

We also found a similarity between the second and third waves. We found that emulation was more likely to occur between dyads that have implemented a similar number of court decisions, suggesting that diffusion seems to occur among states that have either both repeatedly ruled for education finance reform or between states that have both ruled only once (or twice).

In the end we find a very dynamic process of state court involvement in education finance reform. It involves law (including text and precedent), strategic interaction with other branches, the influence of institutional design of the courts (including selection processes), as well as information and emulation of other states and state courts.

What We Want to Know

Of course much work remains, both in understanding the dynamics of education finance reform and state court policy formation and change. For example, we need to know more about legislative dynamics. We need to examine the impact of lobbyists and the introduction of education finance reform measures and how such measures fare in committees.

We also await the introduction of better measures of ideology that allow us to compare state judges with other political actors across time and space of the entire era of education finance reform. We could then match these with existing measures for federal courts and federal legislatures. This would allow us to examine the dynamics of federal and state court interaction in the era predating the seminal 1973 Supreme Court decision.

We also need to examine other state issues of importance, both those that involve some federal oversight in the form of federal constitutional protection and those that are left to the states. In addition, it would nice if we could analyze the process for both salient issues, such as education finance reform, and less salient issues, such as decisions involving state taxation authority and legislation.

Does this same dynamic enfold other issues, salient or nonsalient? Are the dynamics different with federal court authority? We await additional research.

Notes

Chapter 1. Introduction

1. 119 Nev. 460, 76 P.3d 22 (2003).
2. 142 P.3d 339 (2006).
3. Brown v. Board of Education (1954), 493.
4. 163 U.S. 537 (1896).
5. 303 A.2d 273 (1973).
6. 487 P.2d 1241 (1971).
7. 557 P.2d 929 (1976).
8. See http://www.stonybrook.edu/polsci/jsegal/qualtable.pdf.
9. 135 Cong. Rec. S12650-02, *S12650.
10. 554 P.2d 139 (1976).
11. 57 N.Y.2d 127 (1982).
12. 248 Ga. 632 (1981).
13. 790 S.W.2d 186 (1989).

Chapter 2. Why Courts?

1. "Indeed, according to a review of data from the Department of Justice and the National Education Association, many states spend three to four times more per capita on incarceration than on education" (Ogletree 2013, 242). Reinforcing links between poverty, education, and imprisonment furthermore compound problems for less affluent districts (Ogletree 2013).

2. We note the literature that shows courts can send signals to the legislature (see Hausegger and Baum 1999), and this happened with the Nebraska Supreme Court and the Nebraska legislature (Bosworth 2001).

3. For example, while the Kansas Constitution (Kansas Constitution, art. 6, sec. 1) speaks only of "establishing and maintaining public schools," the Idaho

Constitution (Idaho Constitution, art. 9, sec. 1) calls for a "general, uniform and thorough system of public, free, common schools."

4. For a better presentation of the results, we divide the measure by 100, resulting in a possible range from 0 to 1 instead of 0 to 100.

5. According to the US Census 2010, an urban area includes census blocks or block groups that have a population density of at least one thousand people per square mile and with surrounding blocks that have a density of at least five hundred people per square mile. For further information, see https://www.census.gov/geo/reference/ua/uafaq.html.

Chapter 3. Citation Patterns in Education Finance Policy

1. 505 US 577 (1992).

2. 551 US 393 (2007).

3. 335 S.C. 58, 515 S.E.2d 535, 1999 S.C. LEXIS 83 (S.C. 1999).

4. Consider that majority and dissenting opinions in *Parents Involved in Community Schools v. Seattle School District No. 1* 551 US 701 (2007) both claimed they were following *Brown v. Board of Education* 347 US 483 (1954).

5. According to Brandeis's dissent in *New State Ice Co. v. Liebmann*: "It is one of the happy incidents of the federal system that a single courageous State may, if its citizens choose, serve as a laboratory; and try novel social and economic experiments without risk to the rest of the country" (285 US 262 [92]).

6. Keeping with common practice, this definition includes citations broadly, including both positive and negative as well as string citations and more extensive treatments (e.g., Hinkle and Nelson 2016).

7. Here, the pairing is sender: receiver. So, by looking to Idaho: Illinois we would examine those instances where Illinois cites Idaho. Of course, if we were interested in those instances where Idaho cites Illinois, we would need only to look to that particular intersection in our matrix.

8. The diagonal (e.g., A:A, B:B, C:C) is labeled missing as citation or emulation of oneself is not theoretically meaningful in our analysis. These relationships, termed self-loops, are excluded from analysis via statnet.

9. Including the isolates in our graphical depiction of the network would not change the layout of the network or the underlying network statistics in any way. The only difference would be a number of nodes with no edges surrounding the periphery of the network.

10. For example, closeness and eigenvector centrality measure how "near" a given actor is to prominent members in the network. This would be relevant in a friendship network: a relatively peripheral actor who is friends with the social butterfly will have high closeness centrality. In the case of state supreme court citation

networks, this measure is not relevant as it is relatively easy for courts, prominent and marginal alike, to search Lexis for citations without the "introduction" an actor with high closeness centrality can offer. Another type of centrality is betweenness centrality, which ascribes high scores to those actors that sit between two groupings of actors. This can be illustrated in the case of international relations in the Cold War. Since the Swiss maintained diplomatic relations with both the US and Soviet blocs, they could often act as a go-between. Again, the prevalence of Lexis makes this metric less than ideal for our purposes.

11. Unfortunately, the professionalism score is static and does not change across the two waves.

Chapter 4. When Citations Are Not Enough

1. Again, consider that majority and dissenting opinions in *Parents Involved in Community Schools v. Seattle School District No. 1* 551 US 701 (2007) both claimed they were following *Brown v. Board of Education* 347 US 483 (1954).

2. Glynn and Sen (2015), for example, write about differences in judge behavior dependent on whether the judges have daughters. In another example, Epstein et al. (2005) discuss how times of war can influence judicial decisions.

3. 5 Cal.3d 584 (1971).

Chapter 5. Policy Diffusion through Courts

1. The decision established that unequal financing for education did not violate the equal protection clause of the United States Constitution. See chapter 1 for a more detailed description of *San Antonio Independent School District v. Rodriguez* (1973).

2. 5 Cal.3d 584 (1971).

3. 990 A.2d 206; 295 Conn. 240 (2010).

4. In 1996, a California voter initiative legalized marijuana for medical use. Four other states (Oregon, Washington, Alaska, Maine) and DC followed suit in the same decade, eight more joined in the 2000s (Nevada, Montana, Colorado, New Mexico, Vermont, Rhode Island, Michigan, Hawaii). Currently, twenty-eight states and DC have legalized marijuana for medical purposes. Washington and Oregon were the first states to decriminalize small amounts of marijuana for recreational use in 2012. Alaska, Oregon, and DC followed in 2014. California, Maine, Massachusetts, Nevada, and Vermont passed legislation legalizing recreational use of marijuana in 2016, bringing the current total to nine states and DC (https://www.thirdway.org/infographic/timeline-of-state-marijuana-legalization-laws).

5. In some cases, scholars use differences in the sets of characteristics, such as wealth, to measure the similarity between states. In other cases, scholars simply gauge whether individual characteristics of states prompt them to act as leaders/followers (see Shipan and Volden 2007, Volden 2006).

6. For example, the Massachusetts constitutional provision on education is entitled "The Encouragement of Literature, etc.," is 159 words long, and contains lofty goals and aspirations about the importance of education to a free society. Article 8 of the Connecticut Constitution has four sections. While section 1 merely states: "There shall always be free public elementary and secondary schools in the state. The general assembly shall implement this principle by appropriate legislation," section 4 is much more explicit and references justice and equity. The Idaho Constitution, however, is only forty-one words long and speaks of a general right to a free public education.

7. We considered using a duration model to analyze our data (Boehmke, Morey, and Shannon 2006; Box-Steffensmeier and Zorn 2001). Duration modeling has been used often in political science and in the subfield of law and courts (see Langer et al. 2003; Langer 2002; Nixon and Haskin 2000). However, we think a duration model is not appropriate for our interests. Duration modeling seeks to measure the time that elapses before a given event occurs. However, in this study, we are not so much concerned with the time that it takes for adoption of court-ordered finance reform but rather with the probability that a court will emulate another state court and order finance reform premised on a set of shared characteristics.

8. For a discussion of the process, see the appendix in "Empirical Modeling of Policy Diffusion in Federal States: The Dyadic Approach" (Gilardi and Füglister 2008).

9. Note that traditionally in dyadic models the subscript "i" is used for a receiver state, while the subscript "j" is used for a sender state. For ease of presentation throughout this volume we have used "r" to mark a receiver state and "s" to mark a sender state, rather than the more confusing "i" and "j."

10. We recognize that researchers could also model whether states follow other states in not enacting reform. We do not pursue this question within this research.

11. For more information about imitation bias, see Gilardi and Füglister (2008).

12. The specific language Roch and Howard (2008) use is: "For each state constitution, we coded the state as a 1 if the state constitution contained a clause providing for a right to a free public education and a 2 if the section or clause contained specific language on funding or provided for a uniform or efficient funding system" (338). Our maps show the cases brought in the different waves, and table 5.1 shows the particular coding of each state.

13. Individual state policies can be found here: https://nces.ed.gov/blogs/nces/post/financing-education-national-and-state-funding-and-spending-for-public-schools-in-2014 (last accessed September 2018).

14. These measures take into account changes in ideology over time (and thus may have an advantage over other measures, including those developed by Erikson, Wright, and McIver [1989; Wright, Erikson, and McIver 1985; McIver, Erikson, and Wright 1993]). The citizen liberalism scores are based on the congressional roll call voting scores of House incumbents and estimated scores for challengers; these scores are then weighted by the percentage of the vote received in the general election. The governmental liberalism scores are based on the aggregated scores of the estimated ideology of the two chambers of the state legislature and the ideology of the governor.

15. The coefficient in variation is also used by Congress in measuring school finance equity in Title I legislation (Hussar and Sonnenberg 2000).

16. "The formula is: $\dfrac{\left(\dfrac{\sum P_i(M-x_i)^2}{\sum P_i}\right)^{1/2}}{M}$, where P_i = Student enrollment in school district I; x_i = Instructional expenditures per pupil in school district I; and M = Mean instructional expenditures per pupil for all pupils" (Hussar and Sonnenberg 2000, 13).

17. Measures for 1974 to 1979 were calculated using data on instructional expenditures made available through the ELSEGIS Survey of Local Government Finances—School Systems, and coefficients for 1994 to 2004 were calculated using the NCES Local Education Agency (School District) Finance Survey (F-33) Data. For the years 1980 to 1994, the coefficient of variation was obtained from tables made available by the NCES (Hussar and Sonnenberg 2000). Values for the coefficient of variation were interpolated for the years 1976, 1979, 1984, and 1985.

18. Although the Texas legislature has tried over the years to legislate school finance reform, to date it has been unable to do so even with the threat of more state supreme court action (see, e.g., Smith and Todd 2015). As one group of scholars notes, due to the competing urban, rural, and suburban interests as well as the racial and economic disparities within the state, the legislature has not been able to satisfy all litigants and the state courts of their compliance with the court mandates (Imazeki and Reschovsky 2004).

19. We conducted tests examining the levels of multicollinearity in our models. All values were smaller than 10, indicating that a serious level of multicollinearity is not present in our models (Gujarati 2003). All R-squared values (when regressing the independent variable on all other independent variables) were also lower than .9. As a further robustness check, we also dropped the two independent variables with the highest levels of multicollinearity from our models (income for both sender and receiver states), and the results of the models mirror those that we report here.

20. The coefficient estimate could also be interpreted to say that states with legislative reform are more likely to follow other states with legislative reform.

Since we know that it is much more likely for court-mandated reform to occur in states lacking statutory reform, we can assume that diffusion (at least in these early stages) occurs as courts are emulating others that are addressing a policy vacuum.

Chapter 6. Conclusion—How State Courts Move and Change Policy

1. To overturn a constitutional ruling, such as holding that eighteen-year-olds do not have the right to vote in state elections, the Constitution requires a two-thirds vote in each house of Congress and three-quarters of all the states. This happened in *Oregon v. Mitchell* 400 US 112 (1970), which was subsequently overturned by the Twenty-Sixth Amendment to the United States Constitution.

References

Adams, John. 1854. *The Works of John Adams, Second President of the United States: With a Life of the Author, Notes and Illustrations*, vol. 9. Boston: Little, Brown, 1854.

Anderson, Robert. 2011. "Distinguishing Judges: An Empirical Ranking of Judicial Quality in the United States Courts of Appeals." *Missouri Law Review* 76(2): 315–384.

Bailey, Michael A., and Forrest Maltzman. 2008. "Does Legal Doctrine Matter? Unpacking Law and Policy Preferences on the US Supreme Court." *American Political Science Review* 102: 369–384.

Bailey, Michael A., and Forrest Maltzman. 2011. *Constrained Court: Law, Politics, and the Decisions Justices Make.* Princeton: Princeton University Press.

Bartels, Brandon. 2009. "The Constraining Capacity of Legal Doctrine on the US Supreme Court." *American Political Science Review* 103: 474–495.

Beavers, Staci L., and Jeffrey S. Walz. 1998. "Modeling Judicial Federalism: Predictors of State Court Protections of Defendants' Rights." *Publius* 28(3): 43–59.

Bebchuk, Lucian. 1984. "Litigation and Settlement under Imperfect Information." *Rand Journal of Economics* 15: 404–415.

Beck, Nathaniel L., Jonathan Katz, and Richard Tucker. 1998. "Taking Time Seriously: Time-Series-Cross-Section Analysis with a Binary Dependent Variable." *American Journal of Political Science* 42(4): 1260–1288.

Benson, Charles S., and Kevin O'Halloran. 1987. "The Economic History of School Finance in the United States." *Journal of Education Finance* 12(4): 495–515.

Berman, Russell. 2015. "Kansas's Failed Experiment." *Atlantic*, April 9, 2015. https://www.theatlantic.com/politics/archive/2015/04/kansass-failed-experiment/389874/.

Berry, Frances S., and William D. Berry. 1990. "State Lottery Adoptions as Policy Innovations: An Event History Analysis." *American Political Science Review* 84(2): 395–415.

Berry, Frances S., and William Berry. 1994. "The Politics of Tax Increases in the States." *American Journal of Political Science* 38: 855–859.

Berry, Frances S., and William D. Berry. 2014. "Innovation and Diffusion Models in Policy Research." In *Theories of the Policy Process*, edited by Paul Sabatier and Chris Weible, 307–361. Boulder: Westview Press.

Berry, William D., Evan J. Ringquist, Richard C. Fording, and Russell L. Hanson. 1998. "Measuring Citizen and Government Ideology in the American States." *American Journal of Political Science* 42: 337–346.

Blanes i Vidal, Jordi, and Clare Leaver. 2013. "Social Interactions and the Content of Legal Opinions." *Journal of Law, Economics, and Organization* 29(1): 78–114.

Boehmke, Frederick J. 2009. "Policy Emulation or Policy Convergence? Potential Ambiguities in the Dyadic Event History Approach to State Policy Emulation." *Journal of Politics* 71(3): 1125–1140.

Boehmke, Frederick J., Daniel S. Morey, and Megan Shannon. 2006. "Selection Bias and Continuous-Time Duration Models: Consequences and a Proposed Solution." *American Journal of Political Science* 50(1): 192–207.

Boehmke, Frederick J., and Richard Witmer. 2004. "Disentangling Diffusion: The Effects of Social Learning and Economic Competition on State Policy Innovation and Expansion." *Political Research Quarterly* 57(1): 39–51.

Bosworth, Matthew H. 2001. *Courts as Catalysts: State Supreme Courts and Public School Finance Equity*. Albany: State University of New York Press.

Box-Steffensmeier, Janet M., and Bradford S. Jones. 2004. *Event History Modeling: A Guide for Social Scientists*. Cambridge, NY: Cambridge University Press.

Box-Steffensmeier, Janet M., and Christopher J. W. Zorn. 2001. "Duration Models and Proportional Hazards in Political Science." *American Journal of Political Science* 45(4): 972–988.

Boyd, William Lowe, David N. Plank, and Gary Sykes. 2000. "Teachers Unions in Hard Times." In *Conflicting Missions? Teachers Unions and Educational Reform*, edited by Tom Loveless, 174–210. Washington, DC: Brookings Institution Press.

Brace, Paul, and Melinda Gann Hall. 1990. "Neo-Institutionalism and Dissent in State Supreme Courts." *Journal of Politics* 52(1): 54–70.

Brace, Paul, and Melinda Gann Hall. 1995. "Studying Courts Comparatively: The View from the American States." *Political Research Quarterly* 48(1): 5–29.

Brace, Paul, Melinda Gann Hall, and Laura Langer. 1998. "Judicial Choices and the Politics of Abortion: Institutions, Context, and the Autonomy of Courts." *Albany Law Review* 62: 1265–1304.

Brace, Paul, Laura Langer, and Melinda Gann Hall. 2000. "Measuring the Preferences of State Supreme Court Judges." *Journal of Politics* 62: 387–413.

Brennan, William J., Jr. 1986. "James Madison Lecture on Constitutional Law at New York University School of Law on November 18, 1986." Reprinted in "The Bill of Rights and the States: The Revival of State Constitutions as Guardians of Individual Rights." *New York University Law Review* 61: 535–553.

Brennan, William J., Jr. 1977. "State Constitutions and the Protection of Individual Rights." *Harvard Law Review* 90(3): 489–504.

Briffault, Richard. 2006. "Adding Adequacy to Equity: The Evolving Legal Theory of School Finance Reform." *Princeton Law and Public Affairs Working Paper No. 06-013; Columbia Public Law Research Paper No. 06-111*. https://ssrn.com/abstract=906145.

Brimley, Vern, Jr., and Rulon R. Garfield. 2002. *Financing Education in a Climate of Change*. 8th ed. Boston: Allyn and Bacon.

Bush, George H. W. 1991. Address to the Nation on the National Education Strategy, April 18. http://www.presidency.ucsb.edu/ws/?pid=19492.

Caldeira, Gregory A. 1983. "On the Reputation of State Supreme Courts." *Political Behavior* 5(1): 83–108.

Caldeira, Gregory A. 1985. "The Transmission of Legal Precedent: A Study of State Supreme Courts." *American Political Science Review* 79(1): 178–194.

Caldeira, Gregory A. 1988. "Legal Precedent: Structures of Communication between State Supreme Courts." *Social Networks* 10(1): 29–55.

Caldeira, Gregory A., and John R. Wright. 1988. "Organized Interests and Agenda-Setting in the Supreme Court." *American Political Science Review* 82: 1109–1127.

Canes-Wrone, Brandes, Tom S. Clark, and Jason P. Kelly. 2014. "Judicial Selection and Death Penalty Decisions." *American Political Science Review* 108: 23–39.

Cann, Damon, and Teena Wilhelm. 2011. "Policy Venues and Policy Change: The Case of Education Finance Reform." *Social Science Quarterly* 92(4): 1074–1095.

Canon, Bradley C., and Lawrence Baum. 1981. "Patterns of Adoption of Tort Law Innovations: An Application of Diffusion Theory to Judicial Doctrines." *American Political Science Review* 75(4): 975–987.

Carroll, Stephen J., and Rolla Edward Park. 1983. *The Search for Equity in School Finance*. Cambridge, MA: Ballinger.

Casey, Leo. 2006. "The Educational Value of Democratic Voice: A Defense of Collective Bargaining in American Education." In *Collective Bargaining in Education: Negotiating Change in Today's Schools*, edited by Jane Hannaway and Andrew J. Rotherham, 181–294. Cambridge: Harvard Education Press.

Caughey, Devin, and Christopher Warshaw. 2018. "Policy Preferences and Policy Change: Dynamic Responsiveness in the American States, 1936–2014." *American Political Science Review* 112(2): 249–266.

Choi, Stephen, Mitu Gulati, and Eric A. Posner. 2009. "Judicial Evaluations and Information Forcing: Ranking State High Courts and Their Judges." *Duke Law Journal* 58: 1313–1381.

Comparato, Scott A., and Shane A. Gleason. 2013. "Influencing Law from Afar: State Supreme Court Citation Networks." Presented at the Annual Meeting of the Midwest Political Science Association.

Coons, John E., William H. Clune, and Stephen D. Sugarman. 1971. *Private Wealth and Public Education*. Cambridge: Belknap Press of Harvard University Press.

Corley, Pamela C. 2008. "The Supreme Court and Opinion Content." *Political Research Quarterly* 61(3): 468–478.

Corley, Pamela C., Amy Steigerwalt, and Artemus Ward. 2013. *The Puzzle of Unanimity: Consensus on the United States Supreme Court*. Stanford: Stanford University Press.

Cortner, Richard C. 1968. "Strategies and Tactics of Litigants in Constitutional Cases" *Journal of Public Law* 17: 287–307.

Cowen, Joshua, and Katharine O. Strunk. 2014. "How Do Teachers' Unions Influence Education Policy? What We Know and What We Need to Learn." The Education Policy Center at Michigan State University, *Working Paper #42*. https://education.msu.edu/epc/library/documents/WP%2042%20How%20do%20teachers%20unions%20influence%20education%20policy.pdf.

Cranmer, Skyler J., Philip Leifeld, Scott McClurg, and Meredith Rolfe. 2017. "Navigating the Range of Statistical Tools for Inferential Network Analysis." *American Journal of Political Science* 61(1): 237–251.

Cross, Frank B. 2010. "Determinants of Citations to Supreme Court Opinions (and the Remarkable Influence of Justice Scalia)." *Supreme Court Economic Review* 18(1): 177–202.

Culver, John H., and John T. Wold. 1986. "Rose Bird and the Politics of Judicial Accountability in California." *Judicature* 70 (August–September): 80–89.

Desmarais, Bruce A., Jeffrey J. Harden, and Frederick J. Boehmke. 2015. "Persistent Policy Pathways: Inferring Diffusion Networks in the American States." *American Political Science Review* 109(2): 392–406.

Elazar, Daniel. 1966. *American Federalism: A View from the States*. New York: Crowell.

Elazar, Daniel. 1994. *Federal Systems of the World*. 2nd ed. White Plains: Longman.

Elementary and Secondary General Information System (ELSEGIS): Survey of Local Government Finances—School Systems. http://www.icpsr.umich.edu/icpsrweb/ICPSR/studies/2250.

Elkins, Zachary, Andrew T. Guzman, and Beth A. Simmons. 2006. "Competing for Capital: The Diffusion of Bilateral Investment Treaties, 1960–2000." *International Organization* 60(4): 811–846.

Epstein, Lee, Valerie Hoekstra, Jeffrey A. Segal, and Harold J. Spaeth. 1998. "Do Political Preferences Change? A Longitudinal Study of U.S. Supreme Court Justices." *Journal of Politics* 60(3): 801–18.

Epstein, Lee, and Jack Knight. 1998. *Choices Justices Make*. Washington, DC: Congressional Quarterly Press.

Epstein, Lee, Daniel E. Ho, Gary King, and Jeffrey A. Segal. 2005. "The Supreme Court during Crisis." *New York University Law Review* 80: 1–116.

Erikson, Robert S., Gerald C. Wright, and John P. McIver. 1989. "Political Parties, Public Opinion, and State Policy in the United States." *American Political Science Review* 83(3): 729–750.

Erikson, Robert S., Gerald C. Wright, and John P. McIver. 1993. *Statehouse Democracy: Public Opinion and Policy in the American States.* New York: Cambridge University Press.

Evans, William N., Sheila E. Murray, and Robert M. Schwab. 1997. "Schoolhouses, Courthouses, and Statehouses after Serrano." *Journal of Policy Analysis and Management* 16(1): 10–31.

Ferejohn, John, and Charles Shipan. 1990. "Congressional Influence on Bureaucracy." *Journal of Law, Economics, and Organization* 6: 1–20.

Fisher, Patrick, and Travis Pratt. 2006. "Political Culture and the Death Penalty." *Criminal Justice Policy Review* 17(1): 48–60.

Fowler, James H. 2006. "Connecting the Congress: A Study of Cosponsorship Networks." *Political Analysis* 14: 456–487.

Fowler, James H., and Sangick Jeon. 2008. "The Authority of Supreme Court Precedent." *Social Networks* 30: 16–30.

Fowler, James H., Timothy R. Johnson, James F. Spriggs II, Sangick Jeon, and Paul J. Wahlbeck. 2007. "Network Analysis and the Law: Measuring the Legal Importance of Precedents at the US Supreme Court." *Political Analysis* 15: 324–346.

Freeman, Richard B., and Robert G. Valletta. 1988. "The Effects of Public Sector Labor Laws on Labor Market Institutions and Outcomes." In *When Public Sector Employees Unionize*, edited by Richard B. Freeman and Casey Ichniowski, 81–106. Chicago: University of Chicago Press.

Friedkin, Noah E. 1993. "Structural Bases of Interpersonal Influence in Groups: A Longitudinal Case Study." *American Sociological Review* 58: 861–872.

Fuller, Lon L. 1960. "Adjudication and the Rule of Law." *Proceedings of the American Society of International Law* 54: 1–8.

Gambitta, Richard A. L. 1981. "Litigation, Judicial Deference, and Policy Change." In *Governing through Courts*, edited by Richard A. L. Gambitta, Marlynn L. May, and James C. Foster, 259–282. Beverly Hills: Sage.

Garopa, Nuno, and Tom Ginsburg. 2012. "Building Reputation in Constitutional Courts: Political and Judicial Audiences." *Arizona Journal of International and Comparative Law* 28(3): 539–568.

Gibson, James L. 1983. "From Simplicity to Complexity: The Development of Theory in the Study of Judicial Behavior." *Political Behavior* 5(1): 7–49.

Gilardi, Fabrizio, and Katharina Füglister. 2008. "Empirical Modeling of Policy Diffusion in Federal States: The Dyadic Approach." *Swiss Political Science Review* 14(3): 413–450.

Gilardi, Fabrizio, Katharina Füglister, and Stéphane Luyet. 2009. "Learning from Others: The Diffusion of Hospital Financing Reforms in OECD Countries." *Comparative Political Studies* 42: 549–573.

Gillespie, Lauren Nicole. 2009. "The Fourth Wave of Educational Finance Litigation: Pursuing a Federal Right to an Adequate Education." *Cornell Law Review* 95: 989–1020.

Gleason, Shane A., and Robert M. Howard. 2015. "State Supreme Courts and Shared Networking: The Diffusion of Education Policy." *Albany Law Review* 78(4): 1485–1511.

Glynn, Adam, and Maya Sen. 2015. "Identifying Judicial Empathy: Does Having Daughters Cause Judges to Rule for Women's Issues?" *American Journal of Political Science* 59(1): 37–54.

Goldin, Claudia. 1999. "A Brief History of Education in the United States." *Historical Paper 119*. Cambridge: National Bureau of Economic Research.

Graber, Mark A. 1993. "The Nonmajoritarian Difficulty: Legislative Deference to the Judiciary." *Studies in American Political Development* 7(1): 35–73.

Gray, Virginia. 1973. "Innovations in the States: A Diffusion Study." *American Political Science Review* 67: 1174–1185.

Greenhouse, Linda. 2005. *Becoming Justice Blackmun: Harry Blackmun's Supreme Court Journey*. New York: Times Books.

Grossback, Lawrence J., Sean Nicholson-Crotty, and David A. M. Peterson. 2004. "Ideology and Learning in Policy Diffusion." *American Politics Research* 32(5): 521–545.

Gujarati, Damodar N. 2003. *Basic Econometrics*. 4th ed. New York: McGraw-Hill.

Haas, Kenneth C. 1981. "The 'New Federalism' and Prisoners' Rights: State Supreme Courts in Comparative Perspective." *Western Political Quarterly* 34(4): 552–571.

Hall, Melinda Gann. 1992. "Electoral Politics and Strategic Voting in State Supreme Courts." *Journal of Politics* 54: 427.

Hall, Melinda Gann. 2001. "State Supreme Courts in American Democracy: Probing the Myths of Judicial Reform." *American Political Science Review* 95: 315–330.

Hall, Melinda Gann, and Paul Brace. 1999. "State Supreme Courts and Their Environments: Avenues to General Theories of Judicial Choice." In *Supreme Court Decision-Making: New Institutionalist Approaches*, edited by Cornell W. Clayton and Howard Gillman, 281–300. Chicago: University of Chicago Press.

Hammond, Thomas H., and Jack H. Knott. 1996. "Who Controls the Bureaucracy? Presidential Power, Congressional Dominance, Legal Constraints, and Bureaucratic Autonomy in a Model of Multi-Institutional Policy-Making." *Journal of Law, Economics, and Organization* 12(1): 119–166.

Handcock, Mark S., David R. Hunter, Carter T. Butts, Steven M. Goodreau, Pavel N. Krivitsky, and Martina Morris. 2012. *Statnet: Software Tools for the Statistical Analysis of Network Data*. http://CRAN.R-project.org/package=statnet.

Hanna, John. 2016. "S&P Drops Kansas Credit Rating, Citing Ongoing Budget Issues." *AP News*, July 26, 2016. https://apnews.com/c84a2b769df3450590a5e985 9609f834.

Hanushek, Eric A. 1991. "When School Finance 'Reform' May Not Be Good Policy." *Harvard Journal on Legislation* 28: 423–456.

Hausegger, Lori, and Lawrence Baum. 1999. "Inviting Congressional Action: A Study of Supreme Court Motivations in Statutory Interpretation." *American Journal of Political Science* 43: 162–185.

Heise, Michael. 1995a. "State Constitutional Litigation, Educational Finance, and Legal Impact: An Empirical Analysis." *University of Cincinnati Law Review* 63: 1735–1766.

Heise, Michael. 1995b. "State Constitutions, School Finance Litigation, and the 'Third Wave': From Equity to Adequacy." *Temple University Law Review* 68: 1151–1176.

Hill, Kim Quaile, and Jan E. Leighley. 1992. "The Policy Consequences of Class Bias in State Electorates." *American Journal of Political Science* 36(2): 351–365.

Hinkle, Rachael K., and Michael J. Nelson. 2016. "The Transmission of Legal Precedent among State Supreme Courts in the Twenty-First Century." *State Politics and Policy Quarterly* 16(4): 391–410.

Horowitz, Donald L. 1977. *The Courts and Social Policy*. Washington, DC: Brookings Institution Press.

Howard, Robert M., and David C. Nixon. 2002. "Regional Court Influence over Bureaucratic Policymaking: Courts, Ideological Preferences, and the Internal Revenue Service." *Political Research Quarterly* 55(4): 907–922.

Howard, Robert M., Christine M. Roch, and Susanne Schorpp. 2017. "Leaders and Followers: Examining State Court-Ordered Education Finance Reform." *Law and Policy* 39(2): 142–169.

Howard, Robert M., and Amy S. Steigerwalt. 2011. *Judging Law and Policy: Courts and Policymaking in the American Political System*. New York: Routledge.

Huber, Gregory A., and Sanford C. Gordon. 2004. "Accountability and Coercion: Is Justice Blind When It Runs for Office?" *American Journal of Political Science* 48: 247–263.

Hull, N. E. H., and Peter Charles Hoffer. 2001. *Roe v. Wade: The Abortion Rights Controversy in American History*. Lawrence: University Press of Kansas.

Hussar, William J., and William Sonnenberg. 2000. "Trends in Disparities in School District Level Expenditures per Pupil." US Department of Education, Office of Educational Research and Improvement, National Center for Education Statistics. Washington, DC: Educational Resources Information Center.

Imazeki, Jennifer, and Andrew Reschovsky. 2004. "School Finance Reform in Texas: A Never Ending Story?" In *Helping Children Left Behind: State Aid and the Pursuit of Educational Equity*, edited by John Yinger, 251–282. Cambridge: MIT Press.

Johnson, Gbemende. 2014. "Judicial Deference and Executive Control over Administrative Agencies." *State Politics and Policy Quarterly* 14(2): 142–164.

Johnson, Susan Moore, and Susan M. Kardos. 2000. "Reform Bargaining and Its Promise for School Improvement." In *Conflicting Missions? Teachers Unions and Educational Reform*, edited by Tom Loveless, 7–46. Washington, DC: Brookings Institution Press.

Kadushin, Charles. 2012. *Understanding Social Networks: Theories, Concepts, and Findings*. New York: Oxford University Press.

Kane, Thomas J., Stephanie K. Riegg and Douglas O. Staiger. 2006. "School Quality, Neighborhoods, and Housing Prices." *American Law and Economic Review* 8(2): 183–212.

Katzmann, Robert A. 1997. *Courts and Congress*. Washington, DC: Brookings Institution Press.

Kilwein, John C., and Richard A. Brisbin Jr. 1997. "Policy Convergence in a Federal Judicial System: The Application of Intensified Scrutiny Doctrines by State Supreme Courts." *American Journal of Political Science* 41(1): 122–148.

Kingdon, John. 1989. *Congressmen's Voting Decisions*. Ann Arbor: University of Michigan Press.

Klarner, Carl. 2003. "The Measurement of the Partisan Balance of State Government." *State Politics and Policy Quarterly* 3(3): 309–319.

Kluger, Richard. 1975. *Simple Justice*. New York: Random House.

Komesar, Neil K. 1994. *Imperfect Alternatives: Choosing Institutions in Law, Economics, and Public Policy*. Chicago: University of Chicago Press.

Koski, William, and Jesse Hahnel. 2008. "The Past, Present and Possible Futures of Educational Finance Reform Litigation." In *Handbook of Research in Education Finance and Policy*, edited by Helen F. Ladd and Edward B. Fiske, 42–60. New York: Routledge.

Koven, Steven G., and Christopher Mausolff. 2016. "The Influence of Political Culture on State Budgets: Another Look at Elazar's Formulation." *American Review of Public Administration* 73(July): 690–698.

Krehbiel, Keith. 1991. *Information and Legislative Organization*. Ann Arbor: University of Michigan Press.

Krehbiel, Keith. 1996. "Institutional and Partisan Sources of Gridlock." *Journal of Theoretical Politics* 8(1): 7–40.

Kuklinski, James H., and John E. Stanga. 1979. "Political Participation and Government Responsiveness: The Behavior of California Superior Courts." *American Political Science Review* 73(4): 1090–1099.

Langer, Laura. 2002. *Judicial Review in State Supreme Courts: A Comparative Study*. Albany: State University of New York Press.

Langer, Laura, Jody McMullen, Nicholas P. Ray, and Daniel D. Stratton. 2003. "Recruitment of Chief Justices on State Supreme Courts: A Choice between Institutional and Personal Goals." *Journal of Politics* 65: 656–675.

Lefler, Dion. 2016. "Kansas Supreme Court Impeachment Bill Advances in State Senate." *Wichita Eagle*, March 21. http://www.kansas.com/news/politics-government/article67444902.html.

Lovell, George I. 2003. *Legislative Deferrals: Statutory Ambiguity, Judicial Power, and American Democracy*. New York: Cambridge University Press.

Lupu, Yonatan, and James H. Fowler. 2013. "Strategic Citations to Precedent on the U.S. Supreme Court." *Journal of Legal Studies* 42: 151–186.

Madison, James. 1810. "Annual Message to Congress, 5 December 1810." *Founders Online*, National Archives. https://founders.archives.gov/documents/Madison/03-03-02-0059.

Manwaring, Robert L., and Steven M. Sheffrin. 1997. "Litigation, Finance Reform and Aggregate School Spending." *International Tax and Public Finance* 4: 107–127.

Martell, James A. 1977. "School Finance Reform: Robinson v. Cahill." *Urban Law Annual* 13(1): 139–166.

Mayhew, David. 1974. *The Electoral Connection*. New Haven: Yale University Press.

McClosky, Herbert, and John Zaller. 1984. *The American Ethos: Public Attitudes Toward Capitalism and Democracy*. Cambridge: Harvard University Press.

McIver, John P., Robert S. Erikson, and Gerald C. Wright. 1993. "Public Opinion and Public Policy: A View from the States." In *New Perspectives in American Politics*, edited by Lawrence C. Dodd and Calvin Jillson, 249–266. Washington, DC: Congressional Quarterly Press.

Mead, Lawrence M. 2004. "State Political Culture and Welfare Reform." *Policy Studies Journal* 32(2): 271–296.

Meier, Kenneth J., and Deborah R. McFarlane. 1992. "State Policies on Funding of Abortions: A Pooled Cross-sectional Analysis." *Social Science Quarterly* 73: 690–698.

Melnick, R. Shep. 1983. *Regulation and the Courts: The Case of the Clean Air Act*. Washington, DC: Brookings Institution Press.

Merryman, John H. 1954. "The Authority of Authority: What the California Supreme Court Cited in 1950." *Stanford Law Review* 6(4): 613–673.

Minorini, Paul, and Steven Sugarman. 1999. "Educational Adequacy and the Courts: The Promise and Problems of Moving to a New Paradigm." In *Equity and Adequacy in Education Finance: Issues and Perspectives*, edited by H. Ladd, R. Chalk, and J. Hansen, 175–208. Washington, DC: National Academy Press.

Mintrom, Michael, and Sandra Vergari. 1998. "Policy Networks and Innovation Diffusion: The Case of State Education Reforms." *Journal of Politics* 60(1): 126–148.

Moe, Terry M. 2011. *Special Interest: Teachers Unions and America's Public Schools*. Washington, DC: Brookings Institution Press.

Moe, Terry M. 2014. "Teacher Unions and American Education Reform: The Power of Vested Interests." In *The Politics of Major Policy Reform in Postwar America*, edited by J. A. Jenkins and S. M. Milkis, 129–156. Cambridge: Cambridge University Press.

Mooney, Christopher, and Mei-Hsien Lee. 2001. "The Temporal Diffusion of Morality Policy: The Case of Death Penalty Legislation in the American States." In *The Public Clash of Private Values: The Politics of Morality Policy*, edited by Christopher Z. Mooney. Chatham, 170–185. Chatham, NJ: Chatham House.

Mossberger, Karen, and Harold Wolman. 2003. "Policy Transfer as a Form of Prospective Policy Evaluation." *Public Administration Review* 63(4): 428–440.

Mott, Rodney L. 1936. "Judicial Influence." *American Political Science Review* 30(2): 295–315.

Murray, Sheila E., William N. Evans, and Robert M. Schwab. 1998. "Education Finance Reform and the Distribution of Education Resources." *American Economic Review* 88: 789–812.

National Access Network. http://www.schoolfunding.info.

National Center for Education Statistics, US Department of Education. "Common Core Data: Local Education Agency (School District) Finance Survey (F-33) Data." http://nces.ed.gov/ccd/f33agency.asp.

Neal, Zachary. 2014. "The Backbone of Bipartite Projections: Inferring Relationships from Co-Authorship, Co-Attendance and Other Co-Behaviors." *Social Networks* 39: 84–97.

Nechyba, Thomas, and Michael Heise. 2000. "School Finance Reform: Introducing the Choice Factor." In *City Schools: Lessons from New York*, edited by D. Ravitch and J. Vitteritti, 367–392. Baltimore: Johns Hopkins University Press.

Nixon, David C., and J. David Haskin. 2000. "Judicial Retirement Strategies: The Judge's Role in Influencing Party Control of the Appellate Courts." *American Politics Quarterly* 28(4): 458–489.

O'Connor, Karen, and Lee Epstein. 1983. "The Rise of Conservative Interest Group Litigation." *Journal of Politics* 45(2): 479–489.

Ogletree, Charles J., Jr. 2013. "The Legacy and Implications of San Antonio Independent School District v. Rodriguez." *Richmond Public Interest Law Review* 17(2): 515–548.

Olson, Susan. 1990. "Interest Group Litigation in Federal District Court: Beyond the Political Disadvantage Theory." *Journal of Politics* 52(3): 854–882.

Paris, Michael. 2010. *Framing Equal Opportunity: Law and the Politics of School Finance Reform*. Stanford: Stanford University Press.

Pulliam, Mark S. 1999. "State Courts Take Brennan's Revenge." *Wall Street Journal*, January 4, A-11.

Reardon, Sean F., Elena Tej Grewal, Demetra Kalogrides, and Erica Greenberg. 2012. "Brown Fades: The End of Court-Ordered School Desegregation and the Resegregation of American Public Schools." *Journal of Policy Analysis and Management* 31(4): 876–904.

Reed, Douglas S. 1998. "Twenty-Five Years after Rodriguez: School Finance Litigation and the Impact of the New Judicial Federalism." *Law and Society Review* 32(1): 175–220.

Reed, Douglas S. 2001. *On Equal Terms: The Constitutional Politics of Educational Opportunity*. Princeton: Princeton University Press.

Richards, Mark J., and Herbert M. Kritzer. 2002. "Jurisprudential Regimes in Supreme Court Decision Making." *American Political Science Review* 96(2): 305–320.

Roch, Christine, and Robert Howard. 2008. "State Policy Innovation in Perspective: Courts, Legislatures, and Education Finance Reform." *Political Research Quarterly* 6(2): 333–344.

Rogers, James. 2001. "Information and Judicial Review: A Signaling Game of Judicial-Legislative Interaction." *American Journal of Political Science* 45(1): 84–99.

Rosenberg, Gerald N. 2008. *The Hollow Hope*. 2nd ed. Chicago: University of Chicago Press.

Seeljan, Ellen C., and Nicholas Weller. 2011. "Diffusion in Direct Democracy: The Effect of Political Information on Proposals for Tax and Expenditure Limits in the US States." *State Politics and Policy Quarterly* 11(3): 348–368.

Segal, Jeffrey A., and Harold J. Spaeth. 1993. *The Supreme Court and the Attitudinal Model.* New York: Cambridge University Press.

Segal, Jeffrey A., and Harold J. Spaeth. 2002. *The Supreme Court and the Attitudinal Model Revisited.* New York: Cambridge University Press.

Shipan, Charles R., and Craig Volden. 2006. "Bottom-Up Federalism: The Diffusion of Antismoking Policies from US Cities to States." *American Journal of Political Science* 50(4): 825–843.

Shipan, Charles R., and Craig Volden. 2007. "When the Smoke Clears: Interstate vs. Intrastate Diffusion of Youth Access Policies." Presented at the Annual Meeting of the American Political Science Association, Chicago.

Shipan, Charles R., and Craig Volden. 2008. "The Mechanisms of Policy Diffusion." *American Journal of Political Science* 52(4): 840–857.

Smith, Joseph L., and James A. Todd. 2015 "Rules, Standards, and Lower Court Decisions." *Journal of Law and Courts* 3(2): 257–275.

Snyder, Thomas D., and Sally A. Dillow. 2011. *Digest of Education Statistics 2010* (NCES 2011-015). Washington, DC: National Center for Education Statistics, Institute of Education Sciences, U.S. Department of Education.

Solimine, Michael. 2002. "Supreme Court Monitoring of State Courts in the Twenty-First Century." *Indiana Law Review* 35: 335–363.

Songer, Donald R., Charles M. Cameron, and Jeffrey A. Segal. 1995. "An Empirical Test of the Rational Actor Theory of Litigation." *Journal of Politics* 57(4): 1119–1129.

Squire, Peverill. 2008. "Measuring the Professionalism of State Courts of Last Resort." *State Politics and Policy Quarterly* 8: 223–238.

Stoutenborough, James W., and Matthew Beverlin. 2008. "Encouraging Pollution-Free Energy: The Diffusion of State Net Metering Policies." *Social Science Quarterly* 89(5): 1230–1251.

Sutton, Jeffrey S. 2008. "San Antonio Independent School District V. Rodriguez and Its Aftermath." *Virginia Law Review* 94(8): 1963–1986.

Tang, Aaron Y. 2010. "Broken Systems, Broken Duties: A New Theory for School Finance Litigation." *Marquette Law Review* 94: 1195.

Tarr, G. Alan. 1998. *Understanding State Constitutions*. Princeton: Princeton University Press.

Taylor, Jami K., Daniel C. Lewis, Matthew L. Jacobsmeier, and Brian DiSarro. 2012. "Content and Complexity in Policy Reinvention and Diffusion: Gay and Transgender-Inclusive Laws against Discrimination." *State Politics and Policy Quarterly* 12(1): 75–98.

Thro, William E. 1990. "The Third Wave: The Impact of the Montana, Kentucky, and Texas Decisions on the Future of Public School Finance Reform Litigation." *Journal of Law and Education* 19: 219.

Tucker, George. 1843. *Progress of the United States in Population and Wealth in Fifty Years.* New York: Press of Hunt's Merchants' Magazine. https://books.google.com/books?id=xMj-8u5DsgsC&pg=PR5&dq=census+%22United+States%22+1800&as_brr=1#v=onepage&q=census%20%22United%20States%22%201800&f=false.

Unah, Isaac. 2003. "Explaining Corporate Litigation Activity in an Integrated Framework of Interest Mobilization." *Business and Politics* 5(1): 65–94.

Unah, Isaac, and Catherine M. Blalock. 2019. "The Twilight of Brown: Empirical Analysis of Re-Segregation and Voluntary Adoption of School Integration Policies across the United States." *SSRN Scholarly Paper.* https://papers.ssrn.com/abstract=3364021.

Van Slyke, Dora, Alexandra Tan, and Martin Orland. 1994. "School Finance Litigation: A Review of Key Cases." Report prepared for the Education Finance Project. ERIC Institute of Education Sciences. https://files.eric.ed.gov/fulltext/ED394195.pdf.

Verba, Sydney, and Norman H. Nie. 1972. *Participation in America: Political Democracy and Social Equality.* New York: Harper and Row.

Verstegen, Deborah. 1994. "The New Wave of School Finance Reform." *Phi Delta Kappan* 76: 243–250.

Volden, Craig. 2006. "States as Policy Laboratories: Emulating Success in the Children's Health Insurance Program." *American Journal of Political Science* 50(2): 294–312.

Walker, Jack. 1969. "The Diffusion of Innovations among the American States." *American Political Science Review* 63(3): 880–899.

Wang, Jim. 2017. "Here's the Average Net Worth of Americans at Every Age." Wallet Hacks, *Business Insider*, June 5. https://www.businessinsider.com/heres-the-average-net-worth-of-americans-at-every-age-2017-6.

Wasserman, Stanley, and Katherine Faust. 1994. *Social Network Analysis: Methods and Applications.* New York: Cambridge University Press.

Westerland, Chad. 2017. "The Strategic Analysis of Judicial Behavior and the Separation of Powers." In *The Oxford Handbook of Judicial Behavior*, edited by Lee Epstein and Stefanie Lindquist, 253–270. Oxford: Oxford University Press.

Western, Bruce. 1995. "Concepts and Suggestions for Robust Regression Analysis." *American Journal of Political Science* 39(3): 786–817.

Whittington, Keith E. 2003. "William H. Rehnquist: Nixon's Strict Constructionist, Reagan's Chief Justice." In *Rehnquist Justice: Under the Court Dynamic*, edited by Earl M. Maltz, 8–33. Lawrence: University Press of Kansas.

Wilhelm, Teena. 2007. "The Policymaking Role of State Supreme Courts in Education Policy." *Legislative Studies Quarterly* 23(2): 309–333.

Wlezien, Christopher. 2004. "Patterns of Representation: Dynamics of Public Preferences and Policy." *Journal of Politics* 66(1): 1–24.

Wold, John T., and John H. Culver. 1986. "The Defeat of the California Justices: The Campaign, the Electorate, and the Issue of Judicial Accountability." *Judicature* 70: 348–355.

Wood, B. Dan, and Nick A. Theobald. 2003. "Political Responsiveness and Equity in Education Finance." *Journal of Politics* 65(3): 718–738.

Wright, Gerald C., Robert S. Erikson, and John P. McIver. 1985. "Measuring State Partisanship and Ideology with Survey Data." *Journal of Politics* 47(2): 469–489.

Yarbrough, Tinsley. 2008. *Harry A. Blackmun: The Outsider Justice*. New York: Oxford University Press.

Cases Cited

Abbeville County School District v. State 335 S.C. 58, 515 S.E.2d 535, 1999 S.C. LEXIS 8 S.C. 1999)

Board of Education of the Levittown Union Free School District v. Nyquist 57 N.Y.2d 127 (1982)

Brown v. Board of Education 347 US 483 (1954)

Connecticut Coalition for Justice in Education Funding v. Rell 990 A.2d 206; 295 Conn. 240 (2010)

Guinn v. Angle 119 Nev. 460 76 P.3d 22 (2003)

Lee v. Weissman 505 US 577 (1992)

McDaniel v. Thomas 248 Ga. 632 (1981)

Michigan v. Long 463 US 1032 (1983)

Morse v. Frederick 551 US 393 (2007)

Murdoch v. City of Memphis 87 US (20 Wall.) 590 (1875)

Nevadans for Nevada v. Beers 142 P.3d 339 (2006)

New State Ice Co. v. Liebmann 285 US 262 (1932)

Olsen v. State 554 P.2d 139 (1976)

Oregon v. Mitchell 400 US 112 (1970)

Parents Involved in Community Schools v. Seattle School District No. 1 551 US 701 (2007)

Plessy v. Ferguson 163 US 537 (1896)

Robinson v. Cahill 303 A.2d 273 (N.J. 1973)
Rose v. Council for Better Education 790 S.W.2d 186 (1989)
San Antonio Independent School District v. Rodriguez 411 US 1 (1973)
Serrano v. Priest 487 P.2d 1241 (1971)
Serrano v. Priest 557 P.2d 929 (1976)
Texas v. Johnson 491 US 397 (1989)

Index

www.ingramcontent.com/pod-product-compliance
Lightning Source LLC
LaVergne TN
LVHW040157080826
844660LV00001B/5

* 9 7 8 1 4 3 8 4 8 1 3 5 7 *